APPLE WATCH SE

2ND GENERATION

USER GUIDE

The Complete Step-By-Step Instruction Manual For Beginners & Seniors To Master The New Apple Watch SE 2nd Generation. With WatchOS 10 Tips & Tricks.

BY

Williams M. Brown

Table Of Contents

INTRODUCTION

The new Apple Watch SE offers a lot of upgrades over the previous generation in addition to a lot of new functions that Apple claims will be available in the Series 8 (like Crash Detection). Additionally, it outperforms its predecessor by 20% in terms of speed. The GPS version begins at $249/£259, while the cellular version costs $299/£319.

The Apple Watch Ultra and Apple Watch Series 8 are two further new products that Apple has introduced.

Released Date: When Will The New Apple Watch SE Launch

You can place your pre-order for the 2022 Apple Watch SE (now called the SE 2) starting today, September 7, and you'll start receiving it on Friday, September 16.

Apple Watch SE Pricing

The GPS version of the Apple Watch SE 2 starts at $249/£259, while the cellular version costs $299/£319. Whether you choose with the 41mm or 45mm variant the bands or straps you pick will affect the price.

- Price points begin at $249/£259 for the Solo Loop and £259 for the Sport Loop.
- Pricing will increase to $299/£309 due to the Braided Solo Loop.

What's New? How The Apple Watch SE Compares

Are you interested in learning how the new Apple Watch SE stacks up against its predecessor and the Series 8? What follows is essential information:

Design Changes

From what we can see, the 2020 SE 1 and the 2022 SE 2 are visually identical. Get ready to be let down if you were anticipating a completely revamped layout. Its metal construction and standard 40mm or 44mm display are unchanged from previous iterations; however, those seeking a larger display may peruse the Apple Watch Series 8's 41mm or 45mm displays, or the Apple Watch Ultra's 49mm display.

Gold, Silver, and Midnight are the new color options.

Silver, Gold, and Space Grey were the previous color options for the Apple Watch SE.

Series 8 Apple Watches, on the other hand, are available in stainless steel or aluminum. Stainless steel comes in Space Black, Gold, Graphite, and Silver; aluminum colors include Midnight, Starlight, Silver, and Product Red.

Features Of The Apple Watch SE Models

Compared to the Apple Watch Series 8, the new SE2 has a few more functions, but they're not all there. It also has several additional features that were missing from the original model.

Both the SE2 and the Apple Watch Series 8 will include built-in crash sensors. An impact may be detected by the accelerometer. Your loved ones will be notified if you have listed them as emergency contacts and emergency services will be alerted if it detects that you have been in a major automobile collision. It will also provide location information.

Commonalities with the Apple Watch 8 in terms of features are:

- 100 nits brightness
- High and low heart rate and irregular rhythm notifications
- Fall detection
- Crash detection
- Compass Backtrack and redesigned compass app
- 18-hour battery – a low-power mode to extend battery life
- L1 GPS
- W3 wireless chip

Functions that are absent from the Apple Watch SE:

- No Always-On display
- ECG app
- Blood Oxygen app
- Temperature sensing
- Ovulation estimates
- Fast charge
- U1 chip for ultra-wideband

Specs

Apple hasn't made any comparisons to the S7 chip in the Apple Watch 7, so we may presume that the Apple Watch SE 2022's S8 SiP isn't much quicker than that. However, it is 20% faster than the 2020 model.

Price

The Apple Watch SE 2 would replace the Apple Watch 3 as the entry-level model if it is discontinued. Is it going to be cheaper now because of this? At the moment, the 38mm Apple Watch Series 3 costs $199/£179, while the 42mm variant costs $229/£209. The 40mm Apple Watch SE (GPS model) retails for $279/£249 on contract, while the 44mm variant costs $309/£279.

It would be unexpected for Apple to increase the price of the Apple Watch SE if the $199/£179 model were to cease sales. However, similar to the iPhone SE, Apple may introduce a more expensive Apple Watch SE in the future. As reported by LeaksApplePro of iDropNews, Apple is reportedly planning to increase the price of the Apple Watch SE to $299. If Apple keeps selling the older Apple Watch SE, the price of the most affordable Apple Watch may go up much more.

We have compiled a list of the finest Apple Watch sales happening right now in case you would rather not wait for the next version to come out.

Model And Dimensions

With two different screen sizes to choose from, the Apple Watch SE (2020) offers over 30% more real estate than the 38mm and 42mm choices available on the Apple Watch Series 3. Although this is an improvement over the SE, it did cause it to fall behind the Series 7, which had panels that were either 45 or 41 mm thick, a 20% increase.

The following is what you should expect if you were anticipating a bigger screen: According to LeaksApplePro, the 40mm and 44mm sizes will remain unchanged with the Apple Watch SE 2.

Also, a fresh look is not in the cards.

Spec And Features

Regarding the Apple Watch SE 2 (2022), there have been a few verified rumors. Some rumors, nevertheless, have suggested that Apple may upgrade the Apple Watch SE 2 with a new processor, improved sensors, and an always-on display. Continue reading to learn more...

Sensor Enhancements

Already equipped with a bevy of sensors, the Apple Watch SE (2020) monitors your vitals including heart rate, exercise, and sleep while also keeping an eye out for dangers like falls and dangerously loud environments.

Some have speculated that the Apple Watch SE's optical and electrical cardiac sensors would be upgraded in the next version. That is what iDropNews reports, courtesy of LeaksApple Pro.

Adding a temperature sensor to future Apple Watch models is supposedly in the works, although that feature could only make it to the Apple Watch Series 8. This might be useful for monitoring ovulation or identifying fevers.

Always On Display

An issue with the Apple Watch SE (and all Apple Watches until the Series 5) is that you have to lift your arm to activate the display, which is inconvenient since the time isn't always shown.

Once again, LeaksApplePro claims that the Apple Watch SE 2022 model could have an Always On display.

New Processor

When Apple releases new models, one of the first things they often do is replace the CPU to make them faster and more powerful. If the S5 SiP found in the Apple Watch Series 5 is going to carry over to the Apple Watch SE (2020), then the S6 SiP found in the Apple Watch Series 6 should be the one used in the new SE for 2022. Rumour has it that the Apple Watch SE 2022 will supposedly use the same S8 SiP as the Apple Watch Series 8.

Unfortunately, lest you think there's a massive leap in processing power, the S8 is said to be little more than a rebranded S7, which was not all that different from the S6—but it will still be an upgrade.

CHAPTER ONE

HOW TO SET UP YOUR APPLE WATCH

What You Need

A new Apple Watch requires an iPhone XS or later running iOS 17 to be set up and used.

Before You Begin

- Make sure your iPhone is running the most recent version of iOS before you start.
- Verify that your iPhone is linked to a Wi-Fi or cellular network and that Bluetooth is enabled.

Transferring your Apple Watch and its data to a new iPhone is an option if you've previously set it up but would want to use it with a different iPhone.

1. Launch your Apple Watch And Set It To "On" Mode.

When you want to activate your Apple Watch, just press and hold the side button until you see the Apple logo. After that, fasten the watch on your wrist.

2. Keep The Apple Watch Near The iPhone.

After you see the message "Use your iPhone to set up this Apple Watch" on your iPhone, hit Continue. To add a watch to your Apple Watch, launch the app on your iPhone. If you don't see this message, click the All Watches section and press Add Watch.

Select "Set Up for Myself" if you're using your own Apple Watch. Choose "Set Up for a Family Member" instead, and then just follow the on-screen instructions to add a family member's watch to your account.

For the duration of these instructions, keep your iPhone and Apple Watch close to one another.

3. Scroll Through The Animated GIF On Your iPhone

Position the watch face so that it lines up with the iPhone's viewfinder. Your Apple Watch will be linked to your phone when you get a notification.

If you are unable to utilize the camera, the pairing animation may not show, or your iPhone may not be able to read it, try tapping Pair Manually and following the on-screen instructions.

4. Restore From A Previous Backup Or Set Up From Scratch

Choose "Set Up as New Apple Watch" if this is your very first model of Apple Watch. When prompted, install the most recent version of watchOS on your Apple Watch.

A screen labeled "Make This Your New Apple Watch" will display if you have already connected another Apple Watch to your present iPhone. To see the configuration of your new watch with Express Setup, tap on Apps & Data and Settings. Hit Continue after that. Press on Customise Settings if you want to change the default settings on your new watch. After that, choose a prior Apple Watch backup that you would want to restore. Alternately, you may choose to set up your new Apple Watch as a fresh device by tapping the Set Up as New Apple Watch option.

In addition, updating the software on your iPhone may be necessary before you can set up your Apple Watch. Once your iPhone notifies you that an update is ready, you can install it by tapping the Update Now button and then waiting for it to complete.

Select the hand that usually wears your Apple Watch, and then hit Continue.

Press the Agree button after reading the T&C.

5. Use Your Apple ID To Log In.

To access your Apple ID, type in the password prompt. You have the option to sign in later via the Apple Watch app if prompted not to: To sign in, go to General > Apple ID. On cellular Apple Watch models, you'll need to log in to iCloud to use services that rely on a cellular phone number.

An activation lock prompt will appear on your iPhone if Find Me is not already enabled. Your Apple Watch is already associated with an Apple ID if the Activation Lock screen shows. Go ahead and continue setting up by entering the email address and password associated with that Apple ID. To bypass the Activation Lock on an Apple Watch that has been owned before, you may have to get in touch with the prior owner.

6. Create A Passcode

Although passcodes aren't strictly necessary, they are required for some functions, such as Apple Pay. To generate a new passcode on your Apple Watch, first open the Passcode app on your iPhone. Then, choose Create a Passcode or Add a Long Passcode. Press the "Don't Add Passcode" button to bypass this step.

7. Customize Your Settings

Feel free to choose the font size and boldness that suits you best.

Your Apple Watch will display the settings it shares with your iPhone, even if you didn't utilize Express Setup. Features, like Find My, Location Services, Wi-Fi Calling, and Diagnostics, are automatically enabled for your Apple Watch if you've enabled them for your iPhone.

The next step in creating an accurate Fitness and Health profile is to enter or amend personal information such as your date of birth. Noise levels and information regarding Emergency SOS and Fall Detection are among the health warnings that may be enabled.

8. Configure Your Mobile Device And Apple Pay

Settings for cellular are available on Apple Watch models that support it.

Adding a card to your Apple Pay account is the next step. Your iPhone will then show you how to use features like Always On and choose your favorite app view.

To Ensure A Smooth Sync, Keep Your Devices Handy.

Once the pairing process is complete and your Apple Watch is ready to use, the watch face will be shown. For continuous background synchronization, keep your iPhone and Apple Watch near together.

HOW TO UNPAIR AND ERASE YOUR APPLE WATCH

Your Apple Watch will be reset to factory settings if you unpair it.

To Begin

- To unpair your Apple Watch, you'll need the iPhone that connected it. Here are the procedures to take. Along with deleting all data and settings from your Apple Watch, this also disables Activation Lock. Activation Lock will stay even after erasing your Apple Watch from your device, even if you don't have the associated iPhone.
- Before you unpair your Apple Watch and Wallet app, make sure you remove the transportation card from your watch.
- The holes in your Apple Watch casing aren't for a SIM card slot or a reset button; they're for sound transmission to and from the speakers and, on the Apple Watch Ultra, for measuring water depth. Keep anything out of

the openings on your Apple Watch casing to keep it in pristine condition.

How To Unpair And Erase Your Apple Watch If You Have Your iPhone

1. If you want to unpair your Apple Watch from your iPhone, keep the two devices close together.
2. Launch the Apple Watch on your iOS device.
3. Select All Watches from the My Watch menu.
4. To de-pair a watch, tap on the information icon that appears next to it.

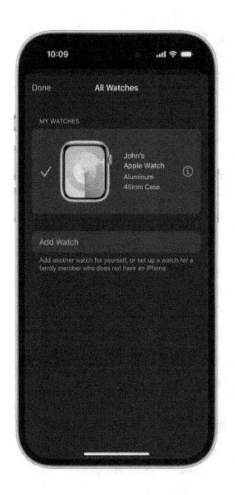

5. Select the Apple Watch and then tap on Unpair.

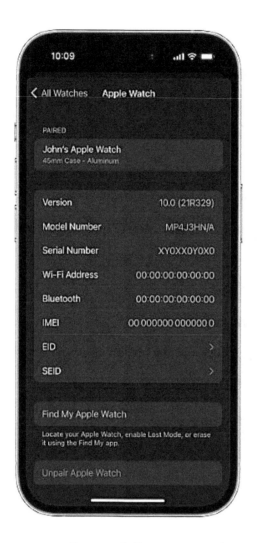

6. Press on "Unpair" next to the name of your Apple Watch.
7. You may opt to retain or cancel your cellular plan with GPS + Cellular models.
   - Retain your plan in case you choose to reconnect your Apple Watch and iPhone.

- Just deactivate your plan if you're not interested in re-pairing your Apple Watch with your iPhone. You may have to get in touch with your cellular provider to terminate your plan if you have no intention of pairing it with any other watches or iPhones.

8. Disabling Activation Lock requires entering your Apple ID password; after that, hit Unpair.

The next time you want to delete everything from your Apple Watch, your iPhone will first make a fresh backup of your device. To transfer data to a different Apple Watch, you may use the backup. The message "Start Pairing" will appear when your Apple Watch unpairs.

To reset your Apple Watch or disable it before selling or giving it away, you may do it now.

How To Erase Your Apple Watch If You Don't Have Your iPhone

1. To erase all content and settings from your Apple Watch, go to Settings > General > Reset.

2. Please enter your password when asked.

3. You have the option to retain or cancel your cellular plan with GPS + Cellular models.

   - Retain your plan in case you choose to reconnect your Apple Watch and iPhone.

   - Just deactivate your plan if you're not interested in re-pairing your Apple Watch with your iPhone. You may have to get in touch with your cellular provider to terminate your plan if you have no intention of pairing it with any other watches or iPhones.

4. To confirm, tap on Erase All. You may return your Apple Watch to its original settings by doing this.

Resetting your Apple Watch is now possible. Disabling Activation Lock requires the Apple ID and password linked to the watch.

Selecting all previous interventions deletes all content, settings, and data stored on your Apple Watch, but it leaves the Activation Lock intact. Unpairing the watch is the first step in removing Activation Lock. A copy of your watch's data is saved on your iPhone before you delete it.

HOW TO UNPAIR AND ERASE APPLE WATCH SETTINGS

To erase all data and settings from your Apple Watch, you have two options:

Take Your Apple Watch Off The Iphone's Charging Dock. This deactivates the Activation Lock, which stops other people from accessing the contents and removes it. If you're thinking about selling or giving your Apple Watch away, do this first.

Wipe Your Apple Watch Clean. While this does remove all data and settings from your Apple

Watch, it will keep it linked to your iPhone. If you want to restart your Apple Watch but want to retain it, this is the way to go.

Take The Apple Watch Apart And Disable The Activation Lock.

1. Launch the Apple Watch on your iOS device.
2. After selecting My Watch, tap All Watches.
3. Unpair Apple Watch may be accessed by tapping the Info button next to your watch.

Now that you've deleted your Apple Watch from iCloud and disabled the Activation Lock, it's ready to be set up again.

Clear All Data From Your Apple Watch

Here are the procedures to delete all data from your Apple Watch without having to unpair it.

1. Go to your Apple Watch's Settings.
2. Enter your passcode after going to General > Reset and tapping Erase All Content and Settings.
3. Your cellular plan is up for grabs if your Apple Watch has one.
   - If you would want to reconnect your Apple Watch and iPhone, be sure to retain your plan.

- To disconnect your Apple Watch from your cellular service or to connect it to another iPhone, just remove your plan. (Try contacting your service provider to terminate your membership.)
4. Once the procedure is complete, you will need to reset your watch. Back up your data and restore it when prompted.

To clear all data and settings from your Apple Watch, you may access this feature on your iPhone by opening the Apple Watch app, tapping My Watch, and then selecting General > Reset.

Important: Resetting your Apple Watch is the only way to access the Settings app if you've lost your passcode.

Cancel Your Mobile Phone Service

At any moment, you may deactivate the cellular plan from your Apple Watch that comes with it.

1. Launch the Apple Watch on your iOS device.
2. To get your cellular plan details, go to My Watch > Cellular > Info.
3. After you've made your selection, tap the "Remove [name of carrier] Plan" button.

Removing this Apple Watch from your cellular plan could require you to contact your provider.

CHAPTER TWO

HOW TO USE APPLE WATCH GESTURES

Not only can you utilize the Digital Crown and side button to communicate with the Apple Watch, but these fundamental movements are also available.

Tap: Touch one finger lightly on the screen.

Swipe: Move one finger across the screen—up, down, left, or right.

Drag: Move one finger across the screen without lifting.

HOW TO ADD MORE APPLE WATCHES TO YOUR ACCOUNT

Multiple Apple Watches may be synced with one iPhone, and you can move between them with ease.

Pair More Than One Apple Watch

The process of pairing your first Apple Watch with another watch is identical. To link your Apple

Watch with your iPhone, just bring your two devices close together, wait for the pairing screen to show on your iPhone, and then hit the link. Alternatively, you might do what I said below:

1. Launch the Apple Watch on your iOS device.
2. Go to the top of the screen and touch on All Watches after tapping on My Watch.
3. After that, just follow the on-screen prompts to add a watch.

Easily Swap Out Your Apple Watch With Another Model.

When you wear an Apple Watch that is already connected, your iPhone will instantly establish a connection with it. Changing your Apple Watch is as simple as raising your wrist.

A manual selection of Apple Watches is also an option:

1. Launch the Apple Watch on your iOS device.
2. Go to the top of the screen and touch on All Watches after tapping on My Watch.
3. Disable Auto Switch and choose an alternative timepiece.

Pressing the side button to activate Control Centre and then looking for the linked status symbol will show you if your Apple Watch is linked to your iPhone.

THE APPLE WATCH APP

You can install applications, change the watch face, modify the settings, and get alerts all via the Apple Watch app on your iPhone.

Launch Apple Watch Mode.

1. Press the Apple Watch app icon on your iPhone.
2. Press the "My Watch" button to see your Apple Watch's settings.

If you're using several Apple Watches with your iPhone, the settings for the one currently in use will be shown.

Swipe to see your watch face collection.

Settings for Apple Watch.

HOW TO CHARGE YOUR APPLE WATCH
Get The Charger Ready.

1. Set your device or charging cord on a level surface in a room with good ventilation.

Included with your Apple Watch is either the Apple Watch Magnetic Charging Cable (for all models) or the Apple Watch Magnetic Fast Charger to USB-C Cable (for Apple Watch Series 7, Apple Watch Series 8, and Apple Watch Series 9 only). A MagSafe Dual Charger or the Apple Watch Magnetic Charging Dock are other options (available separately).

2. The power adapter, which is available separately, must be plugged into the charging wire.
3. Find an electrical outlet and insert the adaptor.

A USB-C power adapter with 18W of output power or more is required for fast charging.

Note: Not all areas provide fast charging.

Get The Apple Watch Ready To Charge.

Set your Apple Watch on its back using either the Apple Watch Magnetic Charging Cable (available with previous versions) or the Apple Watch Magnetic Fast Charger to USB-C cable (included with Apple Watch Series 7 or later). A charging cable's concave end may magnetically attach to your

Apple Watch's rear and ensure that it is in the correct position.

When you start charging your Apple Watch, you'll hear a beep (unless quiet mode is set) and see a charging icon on the face. The Apple Watch power indicator flashes red when the watch is low on juice and green when it's fully charged. A yellow charging icon indicates that your Apple Watch is in Low Power Mode.

Your Apple Watch may be charged by lying flat with the band removed or by placing it on its side.

- To charge your Apple Watch using the MagSafe Duo Charger or Magnetic Charging Dock, just place it on the dock.
- A picture of the Apple Watch Magnetic Charging Cable or Apple Watch Magnetic Fast Charger to USB-C Cable, together with the low battery indication, may appear on the screen if your battery life is critically low.

Apple Watch Series 9

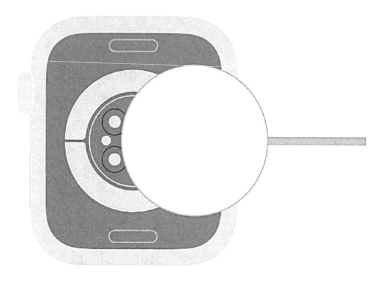

Apple Watch Series 8

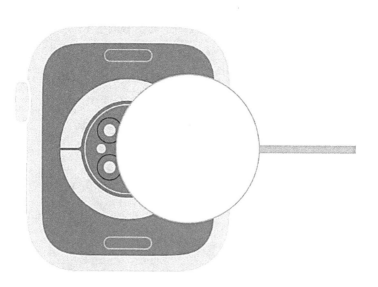

Apple Watch SE (2nd Generation)

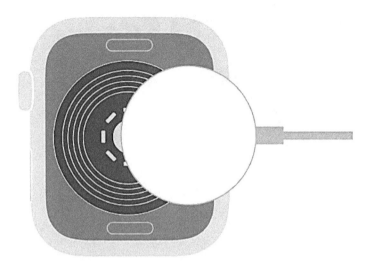

Apple Watch Series 7

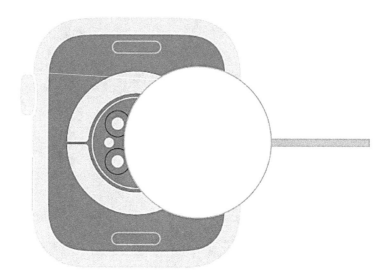

Apple Watch Series 6

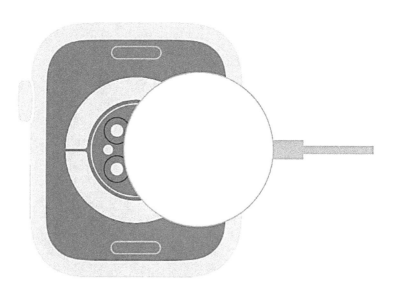

42

Apple Watch SE

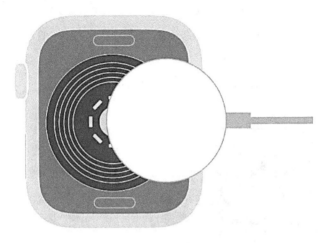

Apple Watch Series 4 And Apple Watch Series 5

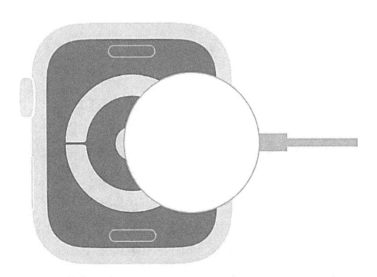

Check Remaining Power

To access the Control Centre and see the remaining battery life, push the side button. You may make checking the battery life easier by including a battery indicator on the watch face.

View the percentage of remaining battery life.

Reducing Energy Use

By using Low Power Mode, you may prolong the life of your battery. When you do this, your heart rate alerts, Always On Display, and background measurements of your blood oxygen levels will be disabled. Notifications from other sources may take longer to arrive, emergency warnings could not get out at all, and certain Wi-Fi and cellular networks have restrictions. Cellular data is disabled until you specifically ask for it, as when you're sending a message or listening to music online.

Important: Once the battery is charged to 80%, Low Power Mode will be disabled.

1. The Control Centre may be accessed by pressing the side button.
2. Next, toggle Low Power Mode by tapping the battery percentage.
3. Scroll down and touch Turn On to confirm your selection.

You have the option to turn it on for one, two, or three days by tapping the Turn On For button.

Hint: To check how much juice is left in your AirPods or other battery-operated item that's synced with your Apple Watch over Bluetooth, hit the battery percentage in the Control Centre. Then, rotate the Digital Crown to see the amount of juice that's left in your headphones.

Your Apple Watch will give you a heads-up and let you switch to Low Power Mode when the battery life gets to 10% or below.

Advice: Check out Apple's Maximising Battery Life and Lifespan pages for further information on how to get the most out of your battery.

Go Back To The Standard Power Setting

1. The Control Centre may be accessed by pressing the side button.
2. To disable Low Power Mode, tap the battery percentage.

Measure The Amount Of Time That Has Passed Since The Battery Was Charged.

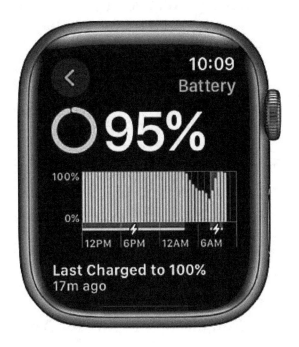

1. Go to your Apple Watch's Settings.
2. Press the Battery button.

   You can see the percentage of battery life left, a graph showing the charge history, and the date and time of last charging all on the Battery screen.

Examine The Condition Of The Battery

Discover how much juice your Apple Watch has left compared to when it was brand new.

1. Go to your Apple Watch's Settings.

2. Select Battery, followed by Battery Health.

Apple Watch notifies you when your battery life is becoming low, giving you the chance to look into your servicing choices.

Charge Batteries More Efficiently

Apple Watch uses on-device machine learning to understand your charging habits and postpone charging beyond 80 percent until you're ready to use it, therefore reducing battery aging.

1. Go to your Apple Watch's Settings.
2. Select Battery, followed by Battery Health.
3. Enable Enhanced Charging for Batteries.

Put An End To Background App Refreshes.

The app you were using before you switched to it won't stay open or use any system resources, but it could "refresh" in the background to see if there are any changes or new material.

Background applications that refresh might use electricity. Disabling this feature will allow you to get the most out of your battery.

1. Go to your Apple Watch's Settings.
2. Navigate to the General menu and choose Background App Refresh.

3. To stop all applications from refreshing, disable Background App Refresh. Another option is to scroll down and disable refresh for certain applications.

Note: Even when you turn off the background app refresh feature, apps that have complications on the current watch face will keep refreshing.

CHAPTER THREE

HOW TO TURN ON AND WAKE APPLE WATCH

You Can Power On And Off Your Apple Watch.

- **Turn On:** If your Apple Watch is currently off, to turn it on, press and hold the side button until you see the Apple logo. There may be a brief period of dark screen before the logo shows.

  When the Apple Watch is turned on, the watch face will display.

  Note: If your Apple Watch is unable to power on, it could be necessary to either charge it or restart it manually.

- **Turn Off:** While it's recommended to keep your Apple Watch on at all times, you may access the power button on the top right, drag the Power Off slider to the right, or press and hold the side button until the sliders display.

Even when your Apple Watch is not in use, you can still see the time by pressing and holding the Digital Crown.

Advice: While your Apple Watch is charging, you cannot power it off. Disconnecting your Apple Watch from its charger is the first step in turning it off.

Always On

If your Apple Watch is compatible with Always On, you can see the time and face even while you're not wearing it. All of the Apple Watch's features activate when you lift your wrist.

Note: Always On is disabled while your Apple Watch is set to Low Power Mode. Press the screen to see the time.

Several Apple Watch models, including the 5, 6, 7, 8, and 9, are compatible with the Always On feature.

1. Go to your Apple Watch's Settings.
2. Select Always On from the Display & Brightness menu.

3. Once Always On is turned on, you may customize the following settings by tapping on them:
    o Select which complications will display data when you let go of your wrist.
    o Select which alerts will display when you put your wrist down to see them.
    o Select which applications will be shown when you rest your wrist on the screen.

Reawaken The Screen Of Your Apple Watch

The following methods activate the Apple Watch screen by default:

- Lift your hand. Your Apple Watch goes back to sleep mode the moment you take your wrist off.
- Press the Digital Crown or tap the screen.
- Press the Digital Crown to the top.

Open the Apple Watch's Settings app. Navigate to Display & Brightness. Disable Wake on Wrist lift and Wake on Crown Rotation if you don't want your Apple Watch to wake up when you lift your wrist or spin the Digital Crown.

Advice: Put your Apple Watch in theatre mode if you want to temporarily disable the wrist-raising feature.

Verify that you choose the correct wrist and watch orientation if your Apple Watch still doesn't wake up when you elevate your wrist. You may need to charge your Apple Watch if it doesn't wake up when you push the screen or use the Digital Crown.

Go Back To The Face Of The Clock

From inside an app, you have the option to set the time until Apple Watch displays the time again.

1. Go to your Apple Watch's Settings.
2. Select Always, After 2 minutes, or After 1 hour as the time you like for your Apple Watch to display the time when you go to General > Return to Clock.
3. Another option is to use the Digital Crown to get back to the face of the clock.

You have the option to define a specific time for each app, but by default, your choice will be applied to all applications. To do this, choose an app from the list, press Custom, and then pick a configuration.

Wake To Your Last Activity

You may configure the Apple Watch to resume your last known location before it slept for certain applications. Audiobooks, Maps, Mindfulness, Music, Podcasts, Now Playing, Stopwatch, Timers, Voice Memos, Walkie-Talkie, and Workout are all part of this category of applications.

1. Go to your Apple Watch's Settings.
2. Scroll down to choose an app, tap on it, and then enable Return to App under General > Return to Clock.

Just quit whatever you're doing in the app—like a podcast, a Maps route, or a timer—to go back to the clock face.

Another option is to launch the Apple Watch app on your iPhone. From there, touch on My Watch. Then, go to General > Return to Clock.

Extended Use Of The Apple Watch Screen

If you want to wake up your Apple Watch with a longer display, you may do that by tapping the screen.

1. Go to your Apple Watch's Settings.
2. To set the wake timer for seventy seconds, go to Display & Brightness, then hit Wake Duration.

HOW TO LOCK OR UNLOCK APPLE WATCH
Decrypt Your Apple Watch

By inputting the passcode, you may manually unlock your Apple Watch. Alternatively, you can configure it to unlock automatically whenever you open your iPhone.

- **Type In The Security Code:** After you wake up your Apple Watch, input the passcode.
- **Lock Your Apple Watch At The Same Time As Your iPhone:** You may enable Unlock with iPhone by opening the Apple Watch app on your iPhone, tapping My Watch, and then tapping Passcode.

  For the Apple Watch to unlock, your iPhone has to be within the Apple Watch's typical Bluetooth range, which is about 33 feet (10 meters). To unlock your Apple Watch while Bluetooth is turned off, just input the passcode on the device.

Advice: It's recommended that you use a separate password for your Apple Watch and iPhone. However, your Apple Watch passcode might vary from your iPhone passcode.

Update Your Security Code

Here are the procedures to alter the passcode you put up when you initially got your Apple Watch:

1. Go to your Apple Watch's Settings.
2. Simply follow the onscreen instructions by tapping Passcode, followed by tapping Change Passcode.

Also, you may access this feature by opening the Apple Watch app on your iPhone. From there, you can access My Watch, touch the Passcode, and finally, hit Change Passcode. Just follow the onscreen instructions.

Hint: To enable a passcode that is more than four digits long, go to your Apple Watch's Settings app, choose Passcode, and then disable Simple Passcode.

Disable The Security Code

1. Go to your Apple Watch's Settings.
2. Select Turn Passcode Off from the Passcode menu.

To disable the passcode, launch the Apple Watch app on your iPhone. Then, go to My Watch, touch Passcode, and finally, go to Turn Passcode Off.

Note: Certain functions may be inaccessible if you choose to deactivate your passcode. For instance, your Apple Watch cannot be used to unlock your Mac or use Apple Pay.

If You're Having Trouble Entering A Basic Passcode Or Have Forgotten It,

If your synced iPhone is being administered by an organization, such as a school or a corporation, you may not be able to use the Simple Passcode or Turn Passcode Off options. Get in touch with the higher-ups at your company.

Lock Automatically

When you take your Apple Watch off, it will lock itself by default. The following steps will allow you to modify the wrist-detecting function.

1. Go to your Apple Watch's Settings.
2. Next, toggle Wrist Detection on or off by tapping the Passcode.

By disabling wrist detection, you may access the following functionalities on your Apple Watch:

- When you double-click the side button on your Apple Watch to authorize a purchase using Apple Pay, you'll be asked to enter your password.

- Certain activity metrics cannot be obtained.
- I have disabled heart rate monitoring and alerts.
- The automatic locking and unlocking of the Apple Watch has been disabled.
- When the Apple Watch detects a hard impact fall, it will not immediately dial 911.

Lock Manually

If you want to lock your Apple Watch by hand, you'll need to disable the wrist detection feature. (To disable Wrist Detection, open the Apple Watch's Settings app, go to Passcode, and then press the option.)

1. The Control Centre may be accessed by pressing the side button.
2. Press the Lock icon.

Your Apple Watch requires you to enter your passcode whenever you want to use it in the future.

If You Forget Your Passcode

Erasing your Apple Watch is the only option if you can't remember your passcode. Several methods exist for this:

- To reset your Apple Watch's settings and passcode, disconnect it from your iPhone. Then, reconnect it.
- Before you can link your Apple Watch with your iPhone again, you must reset it.

Factory Reset Apple Watch After 10 Failed Unlock Attempts

If you want to be sure that your data is safe if your Apple Watch is stolen or lost, you have the option to configure it to wipe all data after 10 failed tries to open it with the incorrect passcode.

1. Go to your Apple Watch's Settings.
2. To enable Erase Data, tap Passcode.

HOW TO CHANGE LANGUAGE AND ORIENTATION ON APPLE WATCH

Pick Your Language And/Or Area

You may choose the language that shows on your Apple Watch if you've configured your iPhone to utilize several languages.

1. Launch the Apple Watch on your iOS device.
2. Navigate to General > Language & Region on My Watch, then hit Custom. From there, choose a language.

Select a language to add by tapping the Add Language button.

Note: The system allows you to select between three terms of address—feminine, masculine, and neutral—in supported languages that employ grammatical gender.

Alter The Position Of The Digital Crown Or The Wrist

You can change your Apple Watch's orientation so that lifting your wrist wakes it up and twisting the Digital Crown moves everything in the way you expect it to if you wish to switch wrists or use the Digital Crown on the other side.

1. Go to your Apple Watch's Settings.
2. Then, choose General > Orientation.

An alternative is to launch the Apple Watch app on your iPhone. From there, choose My Watch, and finally, go to General > Watch Orientation.

HOW TO TAKE OFF, SWAP OUT, AND SECURE BANDS FOR THE APPLE WATCH

When removing, replacing, or tightening bands, follow these basic guidelines.

Use a band that is compatible with the size of your Apple Watch's casing.

- Assuming the sizes are compatible, you can use a band that was made for an earlier Apple Watch model with a band that was made for a later Apple Watch model. This includes Apple Watch Series 1, Apple Watch Series 2, and Apple Watch Series 3.
- There is interoperability between bands that are designed for 38mm, 40mm, and 41mm cases, as well as bands that are designed for 42mm, 44mm, and 45mm cases.
- Any prior version of Apple Watch may be used with most bands made for Series 4, Series 5, Apple Watch SE, Series 6, Series 7, Apple Watch SE (2nd Generation), Series 8, and Series 9.
- For the Apple Watch Series4, Series5, Series6, Series7, Series8, Series9, Apple Watch Series 2nd Generation, and Apple Watch Series SE, there are two bands available: Solo Loop and Braided Solo Loop.

Remove And Change Bands

1. Keep your finger on the Apple Watch's band release button.
2. After removing the band, just slip in the replacement one.

The slot should never be forced onto a band. Keep pressing the band release button if you're still experiencing problems inserting or removing the band.

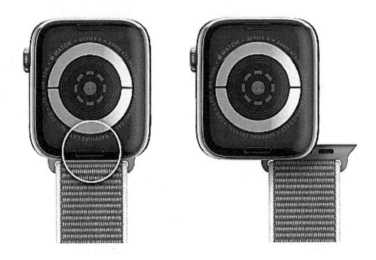

Fasten A Band

Wearing your Apple Watch snugly on your wrist will ensure its best functionality.

For your Apple Watch's heart rate sensor, haptic alerts, and wrist identification to work, the rear of the device requires skin contact. For optimal comfort and sensor performance, ensure that your Apple Watch is snug but not snugger than necessary, allowing some space for your skin to breathe. Furthermore, you may only use the sensors when wearing your Apple Watch on your upper arm.

HOW TO SET UP A FAMILY MEMBER'S APPLE WATCH

For example, if your parent or school-aged kid doesn't have their own iPhone, you may still manage and set up their Apple Watch. This may only be done if you are a parent or guardian in your Family Sharing group, or if you are the family organizer.

To manage settings and update the software, make sure the iPhone you used to connect and set up the Apple Watch is within the usual Bluetooth range of the watch, which is around 33 feet, or 10 meters. The individual you are configuring the Apple Watch for has to be a member of your Family Sharing group and own an Apple Watch SE, Series 4 or later, that can receive cellular data. (The iPhone you use to control your loved one's watch doesn't need to be from the same cellular provider.)

Note: Not all areas provide family setup.

A combination of the Apple Watch app and iPhone's Screen Time allows you to control:

- Safety and the boundaries of communication
- Planned breaks from electronic devices
- Schooltime is an app that restricts access to certain Apple Watch functions when students are in class.
- Account preferences for email and calendar services like Gmail, iCloud, and others
- Discretion settings for private information, explicit material, and purchases

Furthermore, depending on its configuration, you may access the controlled Apple Watch's Activity, Health, and Location data.

Note: There are some limitations to how an Apple Watch configured for a family member may communicate with the iPhone that was used for setup. For instance, you can't transfer tasks from the controlled Apple Watch to the iPhone, and you also can't unlock a linked iPhone using the Apple Watch that you set up for a family member. The iPhone that was used to set up an Apple Watch does not automatically erase apps when you uninstall them from the Apple Watch.

Set Up Your Family Member's Apple Watch

The process of configuring an Apple Watch for a loved one is quite similar to configuring your watch. Before you connect and configure a watch for a loved one, make sure it is empty by erasing all data.

1. Put on your loved one's Apple Watch. Get the perfect fit for your wrist with the Apple Watch by adjusting the band or selecting a band size that suits you.
2. Hold down the side button until the Apple logo shows up to power up the Apple Watch.
3. While waiting for the Apple Watch connection screen to show on your iPhone, bring your iPhone close to the Apple Watch. Then, hit Continue.

   You may also use the Apple Watch app on your iPhone to add a watch. Just launch the app, hit My Watch, then touch All Watches.

4. To add a family member, press Set Up, and then, when prompted, tap Continue.

5. Follow the on-screen instructions to align your iPhone with the Apple Watch via the Apple Watch app's viewfinder. Here, the two devices are paired.
6. Select Apple Watch Settings. To complete setting up your Apple Watch and iPhone, follow the on-screen prompts.

Control The Apple Watch Of A Loved One

1. On the iPhone that is used to control the watch, open the Apple Watch app.
2. To end the process, press Done after selecting My Watch, then Family Watches.

You may access several options, such as these when you touch My Watch on a controlled watch:

Setting	Options
General	Check for updates, change language and region, and reset Apple Watch.
Cellular	Set up cellular if you haven't. See Add Apple Watch to your cellular plan.
Accessibility	Configure accessibility settings.
Emergency SOS	Turn on or off the option to hold the side button to call emergency services, and add and change emergency contacts.
Schooltime	Set up a Schooltime schedule. See Get started with Schooltime.
Screen Time	Manage parental controls, get insights about your family member's screen time, and set limits.
Activity	Manage a fitness experience made for younger users.
App Store	Manage automatic app downloads and updates. See Get more apps on Apple Watch.
Contacts	Choose trusted contacts.
Find My	Choose notification settings.
Handwashing	Manage restrictions, and turn the handwashing timer on or off.
Health	Add or edit health details and Medical ID, view the health data (with the proper permissions and settings) of the person who uses the managed Apple Watch, request to share health data, and choose to stop receiving health data.
Heart	View the heart data (with the proper permissions and settings) of the person who uses the managed Apple Watch, including heart rate, heart rate variability, resting heart rate, and walking heart rate average.
Mail & Calendar	Add a family member's account—Gmail or Outlook, for example. Also choose how often Apple Watch fetches calendar updates.
Messages	Choose dictation options, and edit smart replies.
Noise	Turn Environmental Sound Measurements on or off, and set the noise threshold.
Photos	Select a photo album from the iPhone used to manage the watch, and choose the number of photos Apple Watch can display.
Wallet & Apple Pay	Set up Apple Cash and Express Transit cards.

70

Note: A managed Apple Watch may lack some of the capabilities of an unmanaged Apple Watch. Check out the article "Set up Apple Watch for a family member" on Apple Support.

HOW TO SET UP SCREEN TIME

Make use of Screen Time to set up the Apple Watch's controls for a loved one. You may restrict your family member's access to certain contacts and the applications they use to connect with them, as well as set time limits for when they can't use screens altogether, using Screen Time. Additionally, you have the option to restrict access to explicit material, location data, and apps and the iTunes Store.

This is how you set up Screen Time:

1. On the iPhone that is used to control the watch, open the Apple Watch app.
2. To end the process, press Done after selecting My Watch, then Family Watches.
3. After you've tapped Screen Time, go to Screen Time Settings, and finally, swipe to the on button.
4. Set limitations for apps and websites, as well as controls for permitted material, communication safety, and screen time.
5. Set up a key for Screen Time.

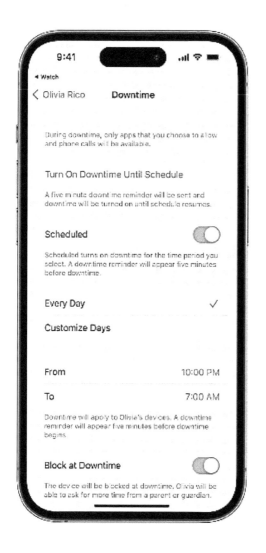

As an alternative, you may access Screen Time in the iPhone's Settings app. From there, you can touch on the name of your family member that appears underneath the Family heading. Then, tap on Turn On Screen Time. Finally, you can adjust the Screen Time settings as you want.

CHAPTER FOUR

HOW TO GET STARTED WITH SCHOOLTIME ON APPLE WATCH

A family member may concentrate on schoolwork by limiting Apple Watch capabilities during school hours.

Schedule Academic Hours

1. On the iPhone that is used to control the watch, open the Apple Watch app.

2. Choose a watch by going to My Watch > Family Watches.
3. After tapping Done, choose Schooltime.
4. After you've enabled Schooltime, tap on Edit Schedule.
5. You may set the watch to activate Schooltime at certain hours and days.
6. For example, if you wish to set up two separate schedules for the same day, one from 8:00 am to noon and the other from 1:00 pm to 3:00 pm, choose Add Time.

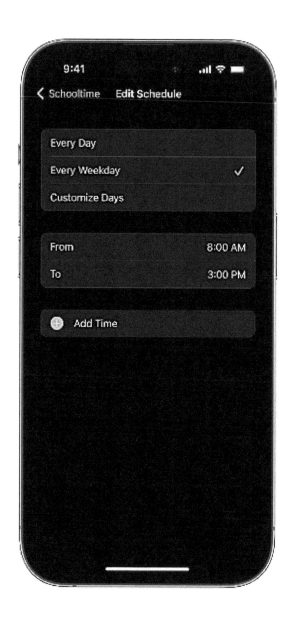

Leave Schooltime

If your loved one has to check their activity rings, for instance, they may briefly leave Schooltime.

If you want to exit, touch the screen, then press and hold the Digital Crown.

The Schooltime face will reappear when you lower your wrist if you leave Schooltime within the allotted hours. Unless you press the Schooltime button in Control Center, or until the next planned start time, Schooltime will not be active during non-scheduled hours.

See When Schooltime Was Unlocked

A report detailing the time and duration of your family member's Schooltime departure will be sent to you after they leave. Here are the procedures to see the report:

1. On the iPhone that is used to control the watch, open the Apple Watch app.
2. Choose a watch by going to My Watch > Family Watches.
3. To see reports for the days, hours, and durations of Schooltime being unlocked, press Done, and then tap Schooltime.

The Apple Watch also displays the report. Launch the Apple Watch's Settings app and then choose Schooltime to see it.

Once the screen shuts off, the school day begins again.

Advice: If your loved one's after-school study group meets outside of regular school hours and they'd prefer not to be interrupted while they work, they may activate Schooltime when it's not in use. To access the Control Center, just hit the side button and then tap the Schooltime button. Simply press and hold the Digital Crown until Schooltime is gone, and then hit Exit. Once the time is set or activated in the Control Center, the school will begin anew.

HOW TO PLAY MUSIC ON A MANAGED APPLE WATCH

Assuming you have a Wi-Fi or cellular connection, your managed Apple Watch can stream Apple Music if you are a member of a Family Sharing group with a family membership.

1. To access the Home screen in the Music app on your controlled Apple Watch, where your music is personalized according to your listening habits, open the app. Also, if you scroll down, you'll see a playlist that the

78

editors at Apple Music put together just for kids and teenagers.

Press the Back button, and then perform one of these things to play music from your collection.

- Press the Radio button to tune in to genre stations and Apple Music Radio.
- To listen to songs stored on your Apple Watch, tap Library.
- Select Search. Then, either write, dictate, or sketch the name of an artist, album, or playlist (on models that allow it; not all languages are supported).

Note: Not all languages are supported by Scribble.

2. To play and choose music, use the controls found in the Music app or the Now Playing app.

HOW TO USE A CONTROLLED APPLE WATCH TO ADD AND PLAY PODCASTS.

On an Apple Watch that is under your control, you can listen to podcasts and watch them online.

Listen To Audio Programs

Start by going to your controlled Apple Watch's Podcasts app. Then, choose an option:

- Choose a podcast to subscribe to from the Home screen.
- For example, you may tell Siri to play "A Frame of Mind" podcast. Listen to the most recent episode of your podcast on your Apple Watch.
- To access your library, use the back button, then choose a program you like to watch.
- You may search for podcasts by tapping the Search button, entering the name of a program, and then tapping on it.

Tap Follow to stay up-to-date on the program. Hit play on an episode.

HOW TO CHECK ACTIVITY AND HEALTH REPORTS FOR FAMILY MEMBERS

You may get records detailing your loved one's activities and medical history if they permit you.

Update The Medical History And Identification Of A Loved One

To input a loved one's medical information or medical ID, please follow these steps:

1. On the iPhone that is used to control the watch, open the Apple Watch app.
2. Choose a watch by going to My Watch > Family Watches.
3. After selecting Done, go to Health, and finally, choose Request [family member's name] Health Data.
4. When you tap Request Health Data, the managed watch will get a notice. Follow these steps once your loved one has agreed to share their health information:
   - To add or change details like your birthday, height, and weight, press the Health Details button.
   - To add emergency contacts and more, tap on Set Up Medical ID.

The medical ID and health data of the person wearing the Apple Watch may be seen on both the iPhone used to control the watch and the watch itself if they have chosen to share this information with you via the Health app.

- **On Your iPhone:** To access a family member's profile, launch the Health app, go to Sharing, touch on their name, and finally, press ().

- **On The Managed Apple Watch:** To get the health information on a controlled Apple Watch, use the watch's Settings app.

View The Medical Records Of A Loved One

You may see more details on your loved one's activities, hearing, daylight, heart rate, and more if they have opted to share their health data.

1. Get the Health app going on your iPhone, and then hit the Sharing button.
2. Under "Sharing With You," tap on the relative's name.
3. First, choose Health Categories from the menu.

HOW TO TRANSFER FUNDS TO ANOTHER APPLE WATCH VIA APPLE CASH FAMILY.

The kids and adolescents in your Family Sharing group may use their Apple Watch to buy things and give and receive money in Messages if you set up Apple Cash as the group administrator. You may lock your child's account, get notifications whenever they make a transaction, and even restrict who they can transfer money to.

Note: Not all areas allow Apple Cash, and it is compatible with iPhone SE and iPhone 6 and newer models.

Establish Apple Cash Family

You must be the designated family organizer to set up Apple Cash Family. Additionally, any family members you want to add must be below the age of 18.

1. Find Family Sharing in the Settings menu on your iPhone.
2. Pick a youngster or young adult, and then hit Apple Cash.
3. Once they've tapped Set Up Apple Cash, they may set up their account by following the onscreen directions.

Within the United States, your loved one can pay for goods and services using Apple Pay, as well as send and receive funds.

Take Charge Of Apple Pay Using A Loved One's Apple Watch

1. To access the watch's financial information, use the Wallet app on the iPhone.
2. Press the More Options option after tapping your Apple Cash card.

3. Below Family, tap on a name.
4. Go ahead and configure these options:
   - Let your loved one decide who they may transfer money to.
   - Set up a notification to be sent whenever a family member makes a purchase.
5. To transfer money with Apple Pay, open the Messages app and tap transfer Money.

To stop a family member from using Apple Pay or giving and receiving money over Messages, tap Lock Apple Cash.

Either launch the Wallet app on your iPhone and then touch your Apple Cash card, or press Transactions on this page to see a family member's transactions. Under "Latest Transactions" and under "Transactions in [year]," you may see the transactions of your family members.

CHAPTER FIVE

HOW TO ORGANIZE APPS ON APPLE WATCH
Switch Up Your App Layout Using Grid View

1. Pressing the Digital Crown on your Apple Watch will take you to the Home Screen.

   To go to grid view from list view, slide down from the top of the screen. Another option is to go to the Apple Watch's Settings app, go to App View, and finally, touch on Grid View.

2. To move an app to a different spot, touch and hold it.
3. Finish by pressing the Digital Crown.

Touch and hold an app, then drag to a new location.

Alternately, launch the Apple Watch app on your iPhone, go to the My Watch section, touch App View, and finally, locate Arrangement. Move the icon of an app by touching and holding it.

Note: The applications in the list view are always shown in alphabetical order.

Touch and hold an app, then drag to a new location.

Remove An App From Apple Watch

Tap the X to delete an app from your Apple Watch after touching and holding the Home Screen. It will also stay on your linked iPhone until you remove it from there.

To delete an app from your Apple Watch, open it in list mode, swipe left on it, and then press the Trash button.

You can be sure that your Apple Watch will likewise get rid of any apps you uninstall on your iPhone. Any program, including those integrated into Apple products, may be restored by downloading it from the program Store on an Apple Watch or iPhone.

Note: Not all applications are erasable from the Apple Watch.

Play Around With The App's Preferences

1. Launch the Apple Watch on your iOS device.
2. To see the applications you've installed, tap My Watch and then scroll down.
3. To modify an app's preferences, touch on it.

Your Apple Watch will also be impacted by some of the limitations that you establish on your iPhone under Settings > Screen Time > Content & Privacy Restrictions. When you turn off the Camera on your iPhone, for instance, the Apple Watch will no longer display the Camera Remote symbol on its home screen.

Verify The Capacity Of Applications' Storage

Your Apple Watch's storage use may be monitored to see how much space is being utilized overall, by apps individually, and how much space is left.

1. Launch the Apple Watch's Settings app.
2. Press on General, then Storage.

To access the storage settings, launch the Apple Watch app on your iPhone. Tap on My Watch, then choose General.

HOW TO GET MORE APPS ON APPLE WATCH

On your Apple Watch, you'll find applications that may help you keep track of time, your health, and your exercise. Whether you're on your iPhone or Apple Watch, you have the option to install third-party applications and access the App Store to get new apps. A unified Home Screen houses all of your applications.

Important: Go to your Apple Watch's Settings, then touch on App Store. From there, enable Automatic Downloads to have the iOS version of any app you've added to your watch downloaded automatically. Your Apple Watch applications will always be up-to-date if you enable Automatic Updates.

Use The App Store To Download Applications To Your Apple Watch.

1. Launch Apple Watch's App Store.
2. Explore highlighted applications and collections by turning the Digital Crown.
3. Touch a collection to see other applications.
4. Click on Get to download a free app. Hover over the price to purchase the app.

If the "Download" button appears instead of a price, it means you have previously bought the software and may download it again at no cost. Having the iOS version of an app installed on your iPhone is often necessary for some applications.

Use the Search button on the top left of the screen to locate a particular app. Enter the name of the app using Scribble or dictation, or type it in (on supported models only; not accessible in all languages). The most popular app categories may be accessed by tapping on a category.

Swipe up from the bottom of the screen and then hit Scribble to utilize it on these same supported devices.

Attention: Cellular data costs can be applicable while using Apple Watch with cellular. There are certain languages that Scribble does not support.

Put Your Existing Iphone Applications Into Action.

If an app on your iPhone is compatible with watchOS, it will be installed immediately and shown on the Home Screen. If you'd rather install just certain programs, here's how:

1. Launch the Apple Watch on your iOS device.
2. To disable Automatic App Install, go to My Watch > General.

3. To access the available apps, press My Watch and then scroll down.

4. Select the applications you want to install, and then tap Install.

HOW TO TELL TIME ON APPLE WATCH

Your Apple Watch has many methods to display the time.

- **Raise your wrist:** Show the time on the watch face, grid view clock, and top right corner of most applications by raising your wrist.

- **Behold The Hour:** Go to your Apple Watch's Settings, then touch on Clock. From there, you may enable Speak Time. You can hear the time by holding two fingers on the face of the watch.

  The Apple Watch also can play hourly chimes. Tap Clock in the Apple Watch's Settings app, and then enable Chimes. To choose either Birds or Bells, tap on Sounds.

- **Feel The Time:** If you want to be able to feel the time on your wrist even while your Apple Watch is in quiet mode, you can do so by opening the Settings app, tapping Clock, tapping Taptic Time, turning it on, and then selecting an option.

Note: You can have Apple Watch constantly tell the time if you deactivate Taptic Time. To enable Taptic Time, go to Settings > Clock and, under Speak Time, toggle Control With Silent Mode.

- Raise your wrist to access Siri and ask, "What time is it?"

HOW TO USE CONTROL CENTER ON APPLE WATCH

You can quickly access a lot of features in Control Center, including checking the battery life, silencing the watch, selecting a Focus, making your Apple Watch a flashlight, switching to Airplane Mode, theater mode, and more.

Control Center May Be Opened Or Closed.

- One press of the side button will bring up the Control Center.
- If the Control Center is open, you may close it by removing your wrist from the screen or by pressing the side button again.

Apple Watch   Apple Watch with Cellular

Icon	Description	For more information
((ᵱ))	Turn cellular on or off—Apple Watch models with cellular only.	See Set up and use cellular service on Apple Watch.
〰	Disconnect from Wi-Fi.	See Disconnect from Wi-Fi.
🧘	Turn on Schooltime—managed Apple Watch models only.	See Set up Schooltime.
((▯))	Ping your iPhone.	See Ping your iPhone (Apple Watch Series 8 and earlier) and Ping and find your iPhone (Apple Watch Series 9 only).
100%	Check your battery percentage.	See Charge Apple Watch.
🔔	Silence Apple Watch.	See Turn on silent mode.
🔒	Lock your watch with a passcode.	See Lock or unlock Apple Watch.
🎭	Turn on theater mode.	See Use theater mode on Apple Watch.
((◉))	Make yourself available for Walkie-Talkie.	See Use Walkie-Talkie on Apple Watch.
🌙	Choose a Focus/Do Not Disturb.	See Create a Focus schedule.
👤	Turn off Personal Focus.	See Create a Focus schedule.

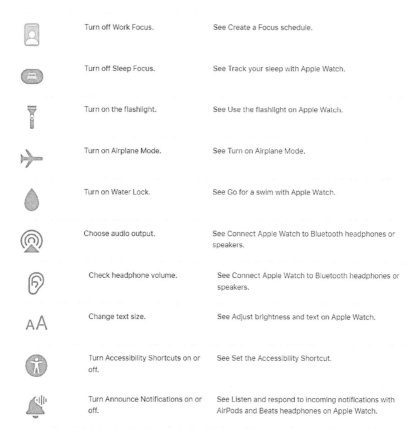

	Turn off Work Focus.	See Create a Focus schedule.
	Turn off Sleep Focus.	See Track your sleep with Apple Watch.
	Turn on the flashlight.	See Use the flashlight on Apple Watch.
	Turn on Airplane Mode.	See Turn on Airplane Mode.
	Turn on Water Lock.	See Go for a swim with Apple Watch.
	Choose audio output.	See Connect Apple Watch to Bluetooth headphones or speakers.
	Check headphone volume.	See Connect Apple Watch to Bluetooth headphones or speakers.
	Change text size.	See Adjust brightness and text on Apple Watch.
	Turn Accessibility Shortcuts on or off.	See Set the Accessibility Shortcut.
	Turn Announce Notifications on or off.	See Listen and respond to incoming notifications with AirPods and Beats headphones on Apple Watch.

Check Control Center Status

At the very top of the Control Center, you'll see a collection of little symbols that represent different settings. For instance, if your Apple Watch is linked to cellular, an app is using your location, and features like Airplane Mode and Do Not Disturb are enabled.

96

Pressing the side button opens the Control Center, where you can see the status icons. Tap the icons to obtain information.

Rearrange Control Center

Following these instructions will allow you to rearrange the buttons in the Control Center:

1. To access the Control Center, press the side button.
2. In Control Center, scroll down to the bottom and hit Edit.
3. Drag a button to a different spot by touching and holding it.

4. Hit the Finish button once you're done.

Disconnect The Buttons On The Control Center

Here are the procedures to remove the buttons from the Control Center:

1. To access the Control Center, press the side button.
2. In Control Center, scroll down to the bottom and hit Edit.
3. To delete a button, tap on its corner and then on the Delete button.
4. Hit the Finish button once you're done.

After removing a button from the Control Center, you may bring it back by opening Edit and tapping the Add button next to the button you want to restore. Hit the Finish button once you're done.

Enable The Airplane Mode.

Depending on the airline, you may be able to travel with your Apple Watch (and iPhone) activated in Airplane Mode. Airplane Mode disables Wi-Fi and cellular (on Apple Watch models that support cellular) while leaving Bluetooth on by default. Turning on Airplane Mode, however, allows you to choose which settings are enabled and disabled.

- **Turn On Airplane Mode On Apple Watch:** Pressing the side button on an Apple Watch will bring up the Control Center. From there, you can hit the Airplane Mode button to enable it.

Turn Airplane Mode on or off.

Siri: "Switch to Airplane Mode," you could say.

- **Turn On Airplane Mode Simultaneously On Your Apple Watch And iPhone:** Go to General > Airplane Mode in the Apple Watch app on your iPhone. After that, touch on My Watch. Finally, enable Mirror iPhone. Switching to Airplane Mode on one device causes the other to do the same if they are within the typical Bluetooth range of each other, which is about 33 feet or 10 meters.

- **Modify The Airplane Mode Settings To Activate Or Deactivate:** Access Airplane Mode on your Apple Watch by opening the Settings app, tapping on Airplane Mode, and then selecting the option to toggle Wi-Fi or Bluetooth on or off automatically.

  If your Apple Watch is set to Airplane Mode, you may access the Settings app and toggle Wi-Fi or Bluetooth on or off by tapping on the corresponding button.

At the very top of the screen, you'll see the Airplane Mode symbol when it's turned on.

Note: Disabling Airplane Mode on both your iPhone and Apple Watch is necessary, even while using Mirror iPhone.

Turn On The Apple Watch's Built-In Light

While maintaining your night vision, you may use the flashlight to illuminate a darkened door lock, signal others that you're going for a run in the dark, or illuminate adjacent items.

- **Turn On The Flashlight:** After opening the Control Center with the side button press, press the Flashlight button to turn on the flashlight. If you want a constant red light, flashing white light, or stable white light, swipe left to pick.

- **Adjust The Brightness:** You may change the brightness by turning the Digital Crown.
- **Turn Off The Brightness:** Either press the side button or the Digital Crown or swipe down from the top of the watch display, to turn off the flashlight.

Switch To Apple Watch's Theater Mode.

When you put your Apple Watch into theater mode, it will remain black since it will not activate the screen when you lift your wrist. Additionally, it disables your Walkie-Talkie feature and puts it on quiet mode, but it still notifies you via haptic feedback.

Once Control Center is activated (by pressing the side button), go to the Theater Mode button and press it.

Turn theater mode on or off.

You can tell if theater mode is active by looking for the status indicator in the upper-right corner of the screen.

While in theater mode, you may wake up your Apple Watch by tapping the screen, pressing the side button or the Digital Crown, or rotating the Digital Crown.

Leave The Wi-Fi Network

From the convenience of Control Center, you may temporarily deactivate your Apple Watch's Wi-Fi connection and switch to using an available cellular data plan. This feature is available on models that support cellular data.

To access the Control Center, press the side button. Then, press and hold the Wi-Fi button.

Tap to disconnect from Wi-Fi.

Leaving the Wi-Fi network causes your Apple Watch to momentarily detach. When you're within range of your Apple Watch's cellular network, the connection will activate. Your Apple Watch will automatically rejoin the Wi-Fi network the next time you go back to the same location unless you've accidentally erased the connection from your iPhone.

Hint: You can access your Apple Watch's Wi-Fi settings by touching and holding the Wi-Fi button in the Control Center.

Turn On Silent Mode

Launch Control Center by pressing the side button; then, choose Silent Mode by tapping the button.

Note: Even in quiet mode, your Apple Watch's alarms and timers will go off while it's charging.

Alternatively, you may access the quiet mode settings by opening the Apple Watch app on your iPhone, tapping My Watch, and then tapping Sounds & Haptics.

Tip: An easy way to silence your Apple Watch whenever it beeps is to put your hand on the screen and hold it there for three seconds. A touch will indicate that mute is enabled. Please activate Cover to Mute on your Apple Watch by going to the

Settings app, tapping Gestures, and finally turning it on.

Send A Ping Message To Your iPhone

You may use your Apple Watch to locate your nearest iPhone.

To access the Control Center, press the side button. Then, press the Ping iPhone button.

So you can find it, your iPhone makes a noise.

Advice: When it's dark? Additionally, your iPhone will flash when you press and hold the Ping iPhone button.

Use Find My on iCloud.com to see whether your iPhone and Apple Watch are within range of one other.

You Can Ping And Locate Your iPhone.

If you have an iPhone 15 nearby, you may utilize Precision Finding on your Apple Watch Series 9 to get instructions for it.

1. Hit the side button on your Apple Watch Series 9 to access Control Center, then hit the Ping iPhone button.

   When your Apple Watch Series 9 is close enough, your iPhone will make a noise and show you the approximate direction and distance to your watch, like 77 feet.

2. Locate it by tapping the Ping iPhone button in the bottom-right corner, or by using your iPhone's built-in sound capabilities.

3. Pay attention to the on-screen heading and make necessary modifications as it advances.

A green light will illuminate your watch screen and two beeps will sound from your iPhone to let you know that it's getting near.

Advice: When it's dark? Additionally, your iPhone will flash when you press and hold the Ping iPhone button.

Use Find My on iCloud.com to see whether your iPhone and Apple Watch are within range of one other.

Note: Not all areas provide Precision Finding.

Reach Out To Your Apple Watch

If you have an iPhone running iOS 17, you may use it to locate your Apple Watch in the area.

1. Get into your iPhone's Settings.
2. Next to Ping My Watch, you should see an Add button; to access it, scroll down to Control Center.
3. You can access Control Center on your iPhone by swiping down from the top right corner. From there, you can hit the Ping Apple Watch button to send a signal to your Apple Watch.

Note: When using the Apple Watch app on an iPhone, the sound will only play on the watch that is chosen under All Watches. This is important to keep in mind if you own several Apple Watches.

Using Find Me, you can also trigger an audio clip on your Apple Watch.

HOW TO USE FOCUS ON APPLE WATCH
Maintaining your present-moment awareness is a key component of effective focus training. With Focus, you can limit interruptions, get just the alerts that are relevant to your current activity, and let other applications and people know that you're working.

Three different Focus modes are available to you: Personal, Sleep, and Work. On the other hand, you may personalize your iPhone's Focus by deciding who can contact you, which applications can notify you, and whether or not time-sensitive alerts are enabled.

Note: If you're using the same Apple ID on several devices, you may make your Focus settings shared by going to Settings > Focus > Share Across Devices.

Activate Or Deactivate A Focus

1. To access the Control Center, press the side button.

2. Tap a Focus after touching and holding the present Focus button.

   Control Center displays the Do Not Disturb button while Focus is not active.

3. Pick an option for Focus—On, On for one hour, or On till tonight/tomorrow morning.

A simple touch of the Focus's Control Center button will disable it.

You can tell when a Focus is on the go because its symbol will pop up anywhere you look—on the watch face, in applications, and Control Center.

Make A Personalized Plan

1. Navigate to Settings > Focus on your iPhone.
2. Select a Focus by tapping the Add button, and then proceed as directed on the screen.

   You have the option to choose a color and an icon to symbolize your unique focus, along with the ability to give it a name.

Pick A Face For Your Focus Watch

When each Focus is engaged, you have the option to show a different watch face. If you're using Work

Focus on your Apple Watch, for instance, you can see the Simple face.

1. Navigate to Settings > Focus on your iPhone.
2. Underneath the picture of the Apple Watch, touch Choose after tapping Focus.
3. Before hitting "Done," choose a watch face.

Make A Routine For Concentration

You may set the times of day for each Focus on Apple Watch, and you can even select to start them at various times of the day. On weekdays, for instance, you may set the Work Focus to begin at 9 in the morning and conclude at 12. Your Focus could be off or a Personal Focus might take over between noon and one o'clock in the afternoon. Then, Monday through Thursday from 1 to 5 p.m., resume the Work Focus.

1. Launch the Apple Watch's Settings app.
2. Choose "Focus," then "Work" or another Focus, and finally "Add new."
3. Simply tap the From and To boxes and provide the start and finish timings for the Focus.
4. Choose the days when the Focus will be active by scrolling down.

5. To preserve the Focus, tap the Back button located in the upper-left corner.

6. You may add more events to the Focus by using this same procedure.

Remove Or Disable A Focus Task

You may deactivate or remove a Focus schedule by doing one of these two things:

- **Disable A Focus Schedule:** You may disable a Focus schedule by going to your Apple Watch's Settings app, tapping Focus, and then tapping on a Focus. Turn off Enabled by tapping a schedule and scrolling down.

Once you would want the schedule to be active again, turn on Enabled.

- **Delete A Focus Schedule:** You may remove a Focus schedule by going to your Apple Watch's Settings, tapping Focus, and finally tapping on a Focus. Find a time slot, touch on it, and then press the Delete button.

HOW TO ADJUST BRIGHTNESS, TEXT SIZE SOUNDS AND HAPTICS ON APPLE WATCH

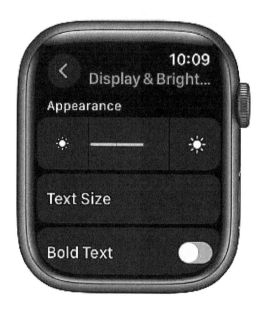

To change the following on your Apple Watch, open the Settings app and then touch on Display & Brightness:

- **Brightness:** To change the brightness, either use the slider or the controls located on the side of the screen, or you may use the Digital Crown.
- **Text Size:** To adjust the font size, swipe left or right on the screen or use the Digital Crown.
- **Bold Text:** Toggle the option to make text bold.

Alternatively, you may use your iPhone to do the same thing. To change the brightness and text size on your Apple Watch, open the app on your iPhone. Then, go to My Watch. From there, hit Display & Brightness.

Adjust Sound

1. Launch the Apple Watch's Settings app.
2. Harps and Taps.
3. Under Alert Volume, you'll find the volume settings. You may also use the slider or the Digital Crown to make adjustments.

An alternative is to access the Apple Watch on an iPhone, go to Sounds & Haptics, and then adjust the Alert Volume using the slider.

Additionally, you have the option to lower the volume of any headphones that are linked to your Apple Watch. Turn on Reduce Loud Sounds in the Sounds & Haptics section of the Headphone Safety app in the Settings app.

Adjust Haptic Intensity

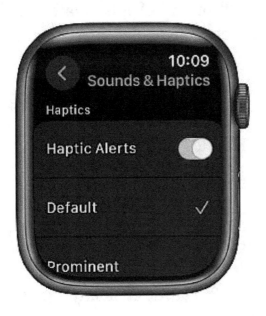

The haptics, or taps on your wrist, that Apple Watch employs to convey warnings and notifications may be fine-tuned.

1. Launch the Apple Watch's Settings app.
2. Select Haptic Alerts from the Sounds & Haptics menu.
3. Pick between Prominent or Default.

On the other hand, you can choose between Default and Prominent in the Apple Watch app on your iPhone. Just launch the app, go to My Watch, and then select Sounds & Haptics.

Toggle The Use Of Digital Crown Haptics.

When you scroll on an Apple Watch using the Digital Crown, you'll hear clicks. Just follow these instructions to activate or deactivate these haptics:

1. Launch the Apple Watch's Settings app.
2. Toggle the switch for Crown Haptics in the Sound & Haptics menu.

    System haptics may also be enabled or disabled.

Another option is to use the Apple Watch app on your iPhone. From there, go to My Watch, then touch on Sounds & Haptics. Finally, toggle Crown Haptics on or off.

Use Taptic Time

You can tell the time on your Apple Watch with a sequence of separate touches even while it's in quiet mode.

1. Launch the Apple Watch's Settings app.
2. Find Taptic Time by tapping Clock and then scrolling down.
3. Select Digits, Terse, or Morse Code as your setting after activating Taptic Time.
   - **Digits:** Your Apple Watch will do a long tap every ten hours, a short tap every hour after that, a long tap every ten minutes, and a short touch every minute after that.
   - **Terse:** Every five hours, your Apple Watch will do a long tap, then every hour after that, it will do a short touch, and finally, every quarter-hour, it will do a long tap.
   - **Morse Code:** Apple Watch uses Morse Code to tap out the time.

The iPhone also can set up Taptic Time. Tap My Watch in the Apple Watch app on your iPhone. From there, choose Clock > Taptic Time to enable the feature.

Note: You can have Apple Watch constantly tell the time if you deactivate Taptic Time. To enable Taptic

Time, go to Settings > Clock and, under Speak Time, toggle Control With Silent Mode.

HOW TO SEE AND RESPOND TO NOTIFICATIONS ON APPLE WATCH

View and reply to notifications on Apple Watch Messages, meeting invites, noise alarms, activity reminders, and other app-generated notifications are just a few examples of how apps can keep you informed. Notifications may be shown on your Apple Watch as they come in, but if you don't have time to read them all at once, they are stored for later.

React Immediately Upon Receiving A Notice

1. Raise your wrist to see any alerts that come your way.

   When the screen is active or not, the notice will appear differently.

   - When the screen is actively shown, a little banner is shown at the top.
   - A notification window fills the screen while the screen is idle.
2. Press on the alert to see it.

3. You may dismiss a notice by swiping it down. Also, you may press Dismiss at the bottom of the notice.

View Messages To Which You Have Not Yet Replied

Notification Center stores any notifications that are unanswered after their first arrival. Any notifications that you have not yet read will be shown by a red dot at the top of your watch face. Just follow these instructions to see it:

1. Swipe down from the top of the watch face to access the Notification Center. To access this from any screen, press and hold the screen's upper corner, and then drag it downward.

   Note: The Apple Watch Home Screen does not allow you to access the Notification Center. Alternatively, you may access the Notification Center by pressing the Digital Crown, which will take you to the watch face or launch an app.

2. To navigate through the list of alerts, either swipe up or down or use the Digital Crown.
3. Press the alert to see it or reply to it.

Hint: Siri may read out loud the alerts in the Notification Center using the speaker on your Apple Watch or Bluetooth headphones. "Read my notifications" is all it takes.

With a left swipe and a press of the X, you may dismiss a notice from the notice Center even before you read it. Navigate to the top of the screen and choose Clear All to erase all alerts.

A group may be opened by tapping on it, and then you can press on a notification to enable group notifications.

Hint: Go into your Apple Watch's Settings, then touch Notifications. From there, you can disable the Notifications Indicator, which will prevent the red dot from showing on the watch face.

Swipe down to view unread notifications.

Turn Off All Alerts On Your Apple Watch

Launch Control Center by pressing the side button; then, choose Silent Mode by tapping the button.

When a notification comes, you may still feel the tap. Here are the procedures to take to avoid tinkling:

1. Once Control Center is launched (by pressing the side button), you may access its features

by tapping the Focus or Do Not Disturb buttons.

2. Pick a choice (On, On for 1 hour, On till this evening/On until tomorrow morning) after tapping Do Not Disturb.

Tip: An easy way to silence your Apple Watch whenever it beeps is to put your hand on the screen and hold it there for three seconds. A touch will indicate that mute is enabled. Verify that Cover to Mute is enabled by opening the Apple Watch's Settings app, tapping Gestures, and finally, turning it on.

CHAPTER SIX

HOW TO MODIFY APPLE WATCH'S NOTIFICATION PREFERENCES

The way you configure app notifications on an Apple Watch will automatically reflect how you do it on your iPhone. Some applications allow you to alter the way alerts are shown.

Note: If you're managing an Apple Watch for a family member, you won't be able to use mirrored settings.

Handle App Alerts In Your Preferred Way.

1. Launch the Apple Watch on your iOS device.
2. Press on Notifications after tapping My Watch.
3. After selecting the app (e.g., Messages), hit Custom, and finally, pick an option. Alternatives might involve:
   - **Allow Notification:** When you enable notifications, the app will show you any new messages in the Notification Center.
   - **Send To Notification Center:** Rather than having your Apple Watch ring or show

the notice, you may choose to have it routed straight to the notice Center.

- **Turn Off Notifications:** so the app doesn't send them.

4. Set the preferred method for categorizing app alerts. Possible choices are:

- **"Off":** means that alerts are not grouped.

- **Without Manual Intervention:** With the use of app data, your Apple Watch can categorize your activities. Your news alerts, for instance, are organized according to the channels you're following, such as CNN, the Washington Post, and People.

- **Grouped By App:** All alerts from the app are compiled here.

Advice: You can customize the alerts you get from certain applications. For instance, under Calendar, you have the option to enable alerts for certain calendars or activities, such as when someone modifies a shared calendar or sends you an invitation. Select which email addresses will be able to get alerts in Mail.

Manage Your Apple Watch's Notifications Without Ever Leaving The Watch.

By swiping left on a notification and choosing the More button, you can easily modify various notification choices right on your Apple Watch. Alternatives might involve:

- Turn off alerts for an hour or all day: Notifications will be transmitted to the notice Center instead of your Apple Watch, so it won't make a sound or show the notice. By swiping left on a notice, tapping the More icon, and then tapping Unmute, you may restore the ability to see and hear these notifications.
- Increase the Summary: On an iPhone, you may see upcoming app alerts in the Notification Summary.

  Get the app to inform you right away again by opening the Settings app on your iPhone, tapping Notifications, tapping the app, and finally tapping Immediate Delivery.

- Even if you're using a Focus that delays most alerts, time-sensitive notifications will always be sent promptly until you turn off time-sensitive. Nevertheless, you may disable the app's ability to send any kind of notification, including time-sensitive ones, by tapping this option.

- Activate: No alerts will be sent by the app. Navigate to the following steps in the Apple Watch app on your iPhone: open the app, hit My Watch, then choose Notifications. From there, select the app whose settings you need to modify, and finally, press Allow Notifications.

Make The Lock Screen Visible For Alerts.

The Apple Watch's lock screen is customizable, so you can decide how alerts show there.

1. Launch the Apple Watch's Settings app.
2. Select Notifications.
3. Please choose one of the following:

- If you want to see a summary of notifications while your Apple Watch is locked, you may turn this feature on. A headline, the name of the alerting app, and its symbol are all part of the summary.
- When you lift your wrist to read a notice, you'll first get a summary. A few seconds later, you'll see the complete contents. To see them all, tap the notification. Take incoming messages as an example; you'll initially see the sender's name before the message itself shows. If you want to hide the whole notice until you touch it, you may turn this setting on.
- Notifications on Wrist Down: When you put your Apple Watch down, notifications normally don't show up. To have alerts shown even when you're not wearing your Apple Watch, enable this feature.

HOW TO USE SMART STACK TO SHOW TIMELY WIDGETS ON APPLE WATCH

When you utilize the Smart Stack—a collection of widgets—at certain points during the day, it will show you the most relevant widgets based on factors like your location, activity, and the current time. If you're going on a trip, for instance, your boarding tickets will appear in the Smart Stack from Wallet, and in the morning, Weather will provide the forecast.

Bring Up The Smart Stack.

1. If the watch face is hidden, press the Digital Crown to reveal it.
2. To access widgets, scroll down using the Digital Crown.

3. Find the widget you want to use, then press it to launch the app that goes along with it.

Note: The Smart Stack's widget with the Music, Workouts, and Messages applications is located at the bottom. Press on an app to launch it.

Widgets May Be Added, Removed, And Rearranged.

When you install the Smart Stack, it comes with a pre-set of widgets that you may customize in any way you want. After you touch and hold the Smart Stack, which is located just below the watch face, you may perform any of the following:

- **Integrate A Widget:** Press the plus sign, then choose an app from the list that shows underneath All Apps or a featured widget. For certain programs, the number of widgets is rather high.
- **Get Rid Of A Widget:** Press the Delete key.
- **Pin And Unpin Widgets:** Widgets may be "pinned" or "unpinned" by tapping the corresponding button on the widget's right side. In the Smart Stack, the pinned widget will show underneath the most recent pinned widget. To make that widget the topmost,

press the Pinned button on the right side of each widget to unpin them.

Upon completion of the Smart Stack editing, tap the Done button.

HOW TO MANAGE YOUR APPLE ID SETTINGS ON THE APPLE WATCH

The data linked to your Apple ID may be seen and modified. You have a lot of options, including the ability to add or amend contact details, change the password, add a trusted phone number, and more.

Edit Personal Information

1. Launch the Apple Watch's Settings app.
2. Choose an option from the following after tapping [your name] on Personal Information:
   - **Change Your Name:** You may sort your name from first to last by tapping on it.
   - **Alter Your Birthdate:** Select "Birthday" and then input a different date.
   - **Sign Up For Announcements, Suggestions, Or Apple News:** Press on the Communication Preferences button. Notifications, apps, music, and TV suggestions, as well as the Apple News Newsletter, may be activated.

Protect Your Apple ID And Password

1. Launch the Apple Watch's Settings app.
2. Select Sign-In & Security after tapping [your name].

   Your Apple ID's linked phone and email accounts are detailed here, along with their respective verification or primary status.

3. Perform one of these tasks:
   - Eliminate A Confirmed Email Address: To remove an email address, tap on it and then press Remove.
   - **Please Provide Our Email And Phone Numbers:** Select the method of contact (email or phone), press Next, provide the desired details, and finally, hit Done.
   - **Log In With A New Apple ID:** Select Change Password and then adhere to the prompts shown on the screen.
   - **You May Edit Or Add A Reliable Phone Number:** To remove a trusted phone number, go to Two-Factor Authentication, touch on your current number, confirm when asked, and then hit Remove Phone Number. If you only have one trusted number, you'll need to add a

new one first. Select Add a Trusted Phone Number to add another trusted number.

- **For Use On Other Devices Or At Icloud.Com, You Will Need To Get A Verification Code:** To get a verification code, go to Two-Factor Authentication and then tap on Go.

- **If An App Or Website Asks You To "Sign In With Apple," You May Change That Option:** After that, choose an app by tapping the "Sign in with Apple" button. If you want to remove the app's association with your Apple ID, tap Stop Using Apple ID. (The subsequent attempt to log in using the app may prompt you to establish a new account.)

- **Protect Your Email Identity:** Select an address and then press Forward To.

This setting lets applications communicate with you without saving your actual email address. By selecting this option, Apple will generate a random email address just for you. Any emails received to this address will be redirected to the personal address you provide.

Verify The Current State Of The Recovery Key: Find out if your Apple ID has a Recovery Key.

One way to make your Apple ID and two-factor authentication even more secure is to use your iOS device to create a recovery key. Your recovery key will allow you to access your Apple ID if you need to reset your password.

See All Of Your Subscriptions And Control Them

1. Launch the Apple Watch's Settings app.
2. Press on [your name].
3. To see your ongoing and expired subscriptions, tap Subscriptions and scroll down.
4. You may examine the price and duration of a subscription, as well as make changes to it, by tapping on it.
5. Exit your subscription by clicking the Cancel Subscription button.

Note: You can't cancel all subscriptions using your iPhone.

When a subscription expires, you may resubscribe by touching the icon and selecting a new subscription period, such as monthly or annually.

View And Manage Your Devices

1. Launch the Apple Watch's Settings app.
2. Press on [your name].
3. To get details on a device, scroll down and touch on it.
4. If the device is unfamiliar, tap Remove from Account.

HOW TO UTILIZE APPLE WATCH SHORTCUTS

With the Apple Watch's Shortcuts app, you can quickly initiate actions with a single touch. You can do a lot more with the shortcuts you make on your iPhone, including making a top 25 playlist or getting directions home fast. The Shortcuts app allows you to launch shortcuts or add them as watch face complications.

Note: Not all iPhone shortcuts will work with the Apple Watch.

Run A Shortcut

1. Start up the Apple Watch's Shortcuts app.
2. Toggle between shortcuts.

Add A Shortcut Complication

1. Press and hold the timepiece until you see the Edit menu.
2. Navigate to the Complications panel by swiping left, and then touch on an issue.
3. Navigate to Shortcuts and choose one.

Enhance Apple Watch With More Shortcuts

1. Launch the iPhone Shortcuts app.
2. Press the "More" button that appears in the upper right corner of a shortcut.
3. To enable the option to display on the Apple Watch, tap the Info button located on the shortcut screen.

HOW TO CONFIGURE APPLE WATCH FOR HANDWASHING

When you begin to wash your hands, your Apple Watch may sense it and prompt you to continue for 20 seconds, the duration suggested by international health agencies.

Turn On Handwashing

1. To activate handwashing on your Apple Watch, open the watch's Settings app.
2. After selecting Handwashing, toggle the Handwashing Timer on.

If your Apple Watch senses that you've begun washing your hands, it will begin a 20-second countdown. It is advised that you complete the work if you do not stop washing within 20 seconds.

Note: Reminders to wash your hands may also be enabled on an Apple Watch that is assigned to a family member. You may enable handwashing reminders and a handwashing timer in the Settings app of the Apple Watch that you are managing.

Launch the Health app on your iPhone. Navigate to Browse > Other Data, and then touch on Handwashing to get a report detailing your typical handwashing durations.

HOW TO CONNECT APPLE WATCH TO A WI-FI NETWORK

Even when you're not near your iPhone, you can still make use of a lot of the capabilities on your Apple Watch by connecting it to a Wi-Fi network.

Pick Out A Wireless Network.

1. To access the Control Center, press the side button.
2. To connect to a wireless network, press and hold the Wi-Fi button until a list of connections appears.

   Only 802.11b/g/n 2.4GHz Wi-Fi networks are compatible with the Apple Watch.

3. Choose an option if the network asks for a password:
   - Password entry is now possible with the Apple Watch's built-in keyboard (on some models only; not all languages supported).
   - The characters for the password may be scribbled on the screen using your finger. Select a capital or lowercase letter with the Digital Crown.
   - Select a password by tapping the Password button.

- Put in the password using the iPhone's keypad.

4. Hit the Join button.

Go For A Private IP Address While Using Your Apple Watch

Every time your Apple Watch connects to a Wi-Fi network, it assigns itself a distinct private address, or media access control (MAC) address, to aid with privacy protection. Stop using a private address for a network if it can't use one for whatever reason (such as providing parental controls or identifying your Apple Watch as permitted to join).

1. To access the Control Center, press the side button.
2. After connecting to a network, you may access its name by touching and holding the Wi-Fi button.
3. Hide the Private Address feature.

Note: All networks that offer Private Addresses should have it enabled for optimal privacy. When you connect your Apple Watch to a private network, it becomes more difficult for other networks to follow it.

Forget A Network

1. To access the Control Center, press the side button.
2. After connecting to a network, you may access its name by touching and holding the Wi-Fi button.
3. Click on the "Forget This Network" button.

If the network asks for a password, you'll have to input it again when you reconnect to it later.

CHAPTER SEVEN

HOW TO CONNECT APPLE WATCH TO BLUETOOTH HEADPHONES OR SPEAKERS

Without having to have your iPhone close by, you may use your Apple Watch to play music on Bluetooth headphones or speakers.

Advice: Just hit play to begin using your AirPods on your Apple Watch once you've connected them up with your iPhone.

Link Wireless Earbuds Or Speakers

To enjoy the majority of the audio on your Apple Watch—including Siri, incoming calls, voicemail, and voice memos—you'll need a Bluetooth speaker or headphones. To activate the exploration mode, follow the on-box instructions for your headphones or speakers. After the Bluetooth device is prepared, proceed as follows:

1. Go to your Apple Watch's Settings and then choose Bluetooth.
2. When the gadget displays, tap on it.

Additionally, the Audiobooks, Music, Now Playing, and Podcasts apps all include AirPlay buttons on their play screens that may be used to access the Bluetooth settings.

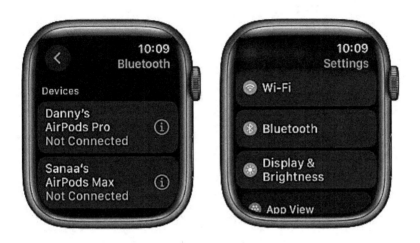

Select A Sound Output Device.

1. To access the Control Center, press the side button.
2. Press the icon for Audio Output, and then choose the desired device.

Listen To Your Headphones And Change The Level.

1. To access the Control Center, press the side button.

2. To adjust the volume of your headphones, press and hold the Headphone Volume button.

   The power level of the headphones is shown via a meter.

3. Adjust the volume by tapping the slider or the settings located under Headphone Volume; alternatively, you may use the Digital Crown.

Decrease The Volume Of Noisy Environments

You may restrict the volume of your headphones to a certain decibel level using the Apple Watch.

1. Launch the Apple Watch's Settings app.
2. Find Headphone Safety under Sounds & Haptics, and then choose Reduce Loud Sounds.
3. Put a level on Reduce Loud Sounds when you turn it on.

Listen To Alerts With Your Headphones Turned Up Loud

The Apple Watch will alert you when you've been listening to too loud music on your headphones for an extended period, and then it will automatically lower the volume to a more comfortable level so that your hearing remains unaffected.

Just follow these instructions to get all the information regarding your headphones' notifications:

1. Launch the Apple Watch's Settings app.
2. To get the last six months of notifications for your headphones, go to Sounds & Haptics > Headphone Safety.

To access the Hearing section of the Health app, open it on your iPhone. From there, choose Headphone Notifications. Finally, touch on a notification.

HOW TO HAND OFF TASKS FROM APPLE WATCH

You can seamlessly switch between devices using handoff, allowing you to keep your concentration intact. For instance, although the Mail app on your Apple Watch allows you to respond to emails, you may find it more convenient to go to your iPhone and use the onscreen keyboard. An Apple Watch that you configure for yourself will have handoff capabilities, but an Apple Watch that you configure for a family member will not. To utilize Handoff, follow these instructions.

1. Get into your iPhone.
2. If your iPhone is equipped with Face ID, you may use the App Switcher by swiping up from the bottom edge and pausing. (If your iPhone has a Home button, you can use the App Switcher by double-clicking the Home button.)
3. Press the button that shows at the screen's bottom to access the identical thing on your iPhone.

Hint: Go to Settings > General > AirPlay & Handoff on your iPhone to enable Handoff if you don't see a button in App Switcher.

By default, handoff is enabled. Launch the Apple Watch app on your iPhone. From there, go to My Watch, then hit General. Finally, toggle off Enable Handoff.

All of the following are compatible with Handoff: Activity, Alarm, Calendar, Home, Mail, Maps, Messages, Music, News, Phone, Podcasts, Reminders, Settings, Siri, Stocks, Stopwatch, Timers, Wallet, Weather, and World Clock. You need to have your Apple Watch and iPhone linked for Handoff to function.

HOW TO SET UP AND USE CELLULAR SERVICE ON APPLE WATCH

You can do a lot more than just make calls and respond to messages when you have an Apple Watch with cellular and a cellular connection to the same carrier as your iPhone. You can utilize Walkie-Talkie, stream music and podcasts, get alerts, and more—all without your iPhone or Wi-Fi.

Note: Not everywhere or with every carrier has cellular coverage.

Upgrade Your Cellular Plan With The Apple Watch.

Just follow the on-screen prompts when you first set up your Apple Watch to enable cellular data. Here are the procedures to activate the service at a later time:

1. Launch the Apple Watch on your iOS device.
2. Navigate to Cellular by tapping My Watch.

To activate cellular for your Apple Watch, follow these steps: find out more about your carrier's service package.

Switch From Your Old Phone Plan To Your New Apple Watch

To move your current cellular plan from one Apple Watch with cellular to another, you need to follow these steps:

1. Start using the Apple Watch app on your iPhone while it's connected to your wrist.
2. To get your cellular plan details, go to My Watch > Cellular > Info.
3. After making your selection, tap the "Remove [name of carrier] Plan" button.

   To deactivate this Apple Watch from your mobile data plan, you may have to get in touch with your service provider.

4. After you've taken off your old Apple Watch and replaced it with your new one that has cellular, go to My Watch and choose Cellular.

   To enable cellular connectivity on your watch, just follow the on-screen prompts.

Initiate Or Deactivate Cellular Data

When your iPhone is close by, it utilizes its network connection. Otherwise, it uses a Wi-Fi network that you have already linked to on your iPhone, or a cellular connection, whichever is optimal for your Apple Watch with cellular. If you want to save battery life, for instance, you may disable cellular data. Just adhere to these guidelines:

1. To access the Control Center, press the side button.
2. Toggle the Cellular feature on or off by tapping the corresponding button.

As soon as your Apple Watch establishes a cellular connection—even when your iPhone is far away—the Cellular button will turn green.

Make Sure The Cell Signal Is Strong.

If you're on a cellular network, try this:

- To see the strength of your cellular signal, choose the Explorer watch face. Four dots make a solid link. Poor one dot.
- Launch the Command Center. You can see the status of your cellular connection in the green bars up above.
- Include the Cellular complication on the face of the watch.

Verify Data Use On Mobile Devices

1. Launch the Apple Watch's Settings app.
2. Press Cellular, and then scroll down to see your data use for the current period.

SAFETY FEATURES ON APPLE WATCH

In case of an emergency, your Apple Watch might come in handy.

- **Show Important Medical Information On Apple Watch:** Create a Medical ID and have it show up on your Apple Watch's lock screen to display crucial medical information. In the event of an emergency, the individuals responding to you will be able to see information about your age, blood type, medical issues, and allergies.

- **Get In Touch With The Paramedics:** To use Siri or Messages, or to contact emergency services, press and hold the side button on your Apple Watch. In the event of an emergency, you may notify loved ones by adding emergency contacts on your phone.

- **When You See A Hard Fall, Call The Emergency Services:** When you activate Fall Detection on your Apple Watch, it may assist you in contacting emergency personnel.

- **In The Event Of A Serious Vehicle Accident, Notify The Appropriate Authorities Immediately:** You can help notify emergency services if your Apple Watch Series 8, Apple Watch SE (2nd Generation), or

Apple Watch Series 9 detects a serious automobile collision.

HOW TO ACCESS YOUR MEDICAL ID INFORMATION ON THE GO WITH APPLE WATCH

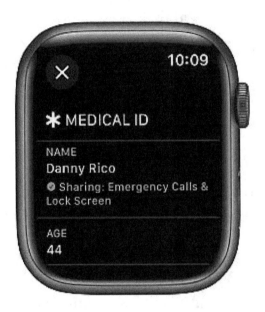

Important medical information, such as your allergies and diseases, may be easily accessed with a medical ID. Your Apple Watch will have access to the same medical records that you enter into your iPhone's Health app. When you dial 911, send a text message, or utilize Emergency SOS (available in the US and Canada only), your Apple Watch may transmit your medical records to the emergency services you've designated.

To ensure that medical personnel have access to your medical ID in the event of an emergency, your Apple Watch can show it.

Just follow these instructions to access your Medical ID on your Apple Watch:

1. The sliders will not show until you press and hold the side button.
2. Move the slider labeled "Medical ID" to the right.
3. When you're done, tap the "Done" button.

An alternative is to access the Apple Watch's medical ID settings via the watch's Settings app.

HOW TO USE YOUR APPLE WATCH TO GET IN TOUCH WITH EMERGENCY SERVICES

You may swiftly summon assistance with the aid of your Apple Watch in the event of an emergency.

Get In Touch With 911 Immediately.

Choose an option from these:

- Slide the Emergency Call slider to the right after pressing and holding the side button until the sliders display.

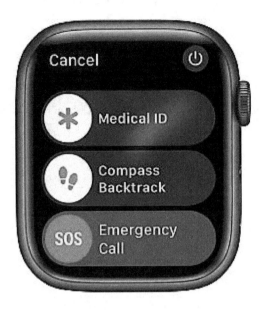

If you're in an area where 911 is available, for instance, your Apple Watch can make that call. (Pressing a keypad number to end the call may be necessary in some countries.)

- Hold down the side button on your Apple Watch until it makes a sound and begins counting down. Your Apple Watch will contact the appropriate authorities as soon as the timer expires. Use the Emergency Call slider to contact emergency services without a countdown if you're in a scenario where you don't want to make any noise since the Apple

Watch will still produce the warning sound even while in quiet mode.

To disable the automatic activation of the emergency countdown upon pressing and holding the side button on your Apple Watch, go to Settings > Automatic Dialling. To disable the Hold Side Button feature, open the Apple Watch's Settings app, go to SOS, and finally, press on Hold Side Button. (Alternatively, you can access the feature via the Apple Watch app on your iPhone. Just launch the app, hit My Watch, then choose Emergency SOS. From there, you can disable the ability to hold the side button.) The Emergency Call slider remains accessible in case of an emergency.

- Just tell Siri to dial 911.
- To dial 911 from your Apple Watch, open the Messages app, choose New Message, then select Add Contact. Then, press the number pad button and enter 911. Select Create Message, type in your message, and then hit the Send button.

After detecting a heavy fall, your Apple Watch will try to automatically contact emergency services if you have remained motionless for about one minute and Fall Detection is enabled.

After 20 seconds, your Apple Watch will show an alarm and may start calling for help if it detects a serious automobile collision.

Assuming cellular service is available, you may make an emergency call using the cellular versions of the following Apple Watch models: Series 5, Apple Watch SE, Series 6, Apple Watch Series 7, Apple Watch Series 8, or Apple Watch Series 9. If your Apple Watch isn't activated, doesn't work with a certain cellular network, isn't configured to receive emergency calls, or isn't set up for cellular service, some cellular networks might reject an emergency call from your Apple Watch Series 5, Apple Watch SE, Apple Watch Series 6, Apple Watch Series 7, Apple Watch Series 8, or Apple Watch Series 9.

Additional contacts for emergencies may be added. Your Apple Watch will send a text message to your emergency contacts and active Check-In contact as soon as an emergency call concludes unless you decide to stop the action. For a certain amount of time, after you activate SOS mode, your emergency contacts and active Check-in contacts will get location updates from your Apple Watch whenever your location changes.

When you initiate an Emergency SOS call while overseas, your watch will link to the local emergency services, but it will not notify your emergency contacts of your position or send them a text message. Even without cellular connectivity, your watch can still make international emergency calls in some areas.

Terminate A Life-Threatening Call

If you happen to have accidentally begun an emergency call, just hit the End Call button to terminate.

Keep Your Emergency Contact Information Up To Date.

You will be taken to your emergency address if the emergency personnel are unable to find you.

1. Get into your iPhone's Settings.
2. Tap Update Emergency Address under the Phone app's Wi-Fi Calling settings, and then input your emergency contact information.

HOW TO MANAGE FALL DETECTION ON APPLE WATCH

If you've activated Apple Watch's Fall Detection feature, it will notify your emergency contacts and link you to emergency services in the event of a heavy fall. If your Apple Watch senses that you've remained motionless for around one minute after a violent fall, it will tap your wrist, make an alert sound, and try to contact emergency personnel.

If you want to contact emergency services, you'll need an iPhone or Apple Watch that is either connected to a cellular network or has Wi-Fi calling enabled and accessible.

When cellular and Wi-Fi connectivity is unavailable and your Apple Watch is in range of your iPhone 14 or later, Fall Detection will use your iPhone to transmit the alert using Emergency SOS via satellite, if such a feature is available.

Fall Detection is on automatically if the birthdate you specify when configuring your Apple Watch (or adding it to the Health app on iPhone) shows that you are 55 or older. To manually activate Fall Detection, follow these steps if you are between the ages of 18 and 55:

1. Go to your Apple Watch's Settings.
2. Select SOS > Fall Detection and toggle it on.

   Alternatively, you may activate Fall Detection by opening the Apple Watch app on your iPhone, tapping My Watch, and then selecting Emergency SOS.

Note: Even after detecting a heavy impact fall, Apple Watch will not automatically try to contact emergency services if you are off wrist detection.

3. Pick "Always on" if you want Fall Detection enabled always, or "Only on during workouts" if you want it to activate just when you begin an exercise.

Fall Detection is enabled by default during workouts on new Apple Watches purchased by users between the ages of 18 and 55 and running watchOS 8.1 or later. To activate the "Only on during workouts" setting on an upgraded Apple Watch running a previous version of watchOS, you'll need to go into the settings and find that option.

CHAPTER EIGHT

HOW TO MANAGE CRASH DETECTION ON APPLE WATCH

Your Apple Watch may assist you connect to emergency services and inform your emergency contacts if it detects a major automobile collision, whether it's a Series 8, Series 9, or Apple Watch SE (2nd Generation).

After 20 seconds of notifying you of a serious vehicle accident, your Apple Watch will begin dialing 911 until you tell it to stop. If you do not respond, an audio message will be played for the benefit of emergency services. This message will apprise them of the seriousness of the automobile collision to which you have been a victim and will provide them with your precise location and a rough idea of the search radius.

If you want to contact emergency services, you'll need an iPhone or Apple Watch that is either connected to a cellular network or has Wi-Fi calling enabled and `accessible.

Crash Detection alerts to emergency services may be conveyed using the Emergency SOS via satellite system if cellular and Wi-Fi coverage is unavailable and your Apple Watch is near your iPhone 14 or later. This feature is accessible in areas where Emergency SOS via satellite is available.

Note: Incident Detection will not supersede any preexisting emergency calls made via other methods in the event of a serious vehicle incident.

Enable Or Disable Crash Detection

Default, Crash Detection is set to on. After a serious vehicle accident, you may disable Apple's warnings and automated emergency calls by following these steps:

1. Go to your Apple Watch's Settings.
2. Turn off the feature that alerts you when a crash occurs by going to SOS > Crash Detection.

Attention: Not all automotive accidents can be detected by Apple Watch.

HOW TO USE SIRI ON APPLE WATCH
Practical Siri Voice Controls

Your Apple Watch may become an extension of your phone with the help of Siri. For instance, after asking a broad query, Siri will show you the top search results with a short clip from each page, translate what you say into another language, or identify a music and give you an immediate Shazam result. With a simple touch, you may access the website on your Apple Watch. If you often have to accomplish activities that require a few steps, try utilizing Siri instead.

Siri isn't localized to every country or language.

Siri: What would you say?

- "How does one express the question 'How are you?' in Chinese?"
- "Go for a run outside for thirty minutes."
- "Please inform Kathleen that I am nearly done."
- "Start the Sleep app."
- "Access Preferences"
- I don't know the music.
- "How do rainbows form?"
- "Where am I now?"
- "What are some possible questions I could ask you?"

How To Use Siri

You may ask Siri anything by doing one of the following:

- Pull up your Apple Watch and start speaking.

  Navigate to the Settings app on your Apple Watch, then choose Siri. From there, disable Raise to Speak.

- Simply say "Hey Siri" or "Siri" and then ask for what you want.

To disable "Ask Siri," go to your Apple Watch's Settings app, then touch Siri. From there, choose Listen for "Siri" or "Hey Siri," and finally, pick Off.

Note: Not all languages and areas support the usage of "Siri" exclusively.

- Once the listening indication appears, voice your request while pressing and holding the Digital Crown.

To disable the Press Digital Crown function, go to your Apple Watch's Settings, go to Siri, and finally, touch on the functionality.

Tip: You may let go of your wrist after you've activated Siri. When there's a reply, you'll hear a tap.

While holding down the Digital Crown, you may ask Siri a question or carry on the discussion.

Just like on iOS, iPadOS, and macOS, Siri can talk back to you. If you have a Bluetooth headset or speakers that are linked to your Apple Watch, you can also listen to Siri's replies that way.

Note: You'll need an internet connection for Siri to work on your Apple Watch. Cellular fees could be applicable.

Customise Siri's Responses

On an Apple Watch, Siri can utter replies. Launch the Apple Watch's Settings app. From there, go to Siri. Tap on Siri Responses. From the list that appears, select:

- Siri is always on, even in quiet mode on your Apple Watch.
- When you put your Apple Watch into quiet mode, Siri will not respond.
- Only when your Apple Watch is linked to Bluetooth headphones can Siri voice replies.

Navigate to the Settings app on your Apple Watch, then choose Siri. From there, choose Language or Siri Voice to customize the language and voice used by Siri. You may choose a new speech type by tapping Siri speech.

Note: Not all languages have the ability to modify Siri's voice.

Make Your Siri Commands Visible With Subtitles And Transcripts

Siri captions and transcriptions of your queries and replies may be shown on your Apple Watch. To toggle Always Show Siri Captions and Always Show Speech on or off, go to the Apple Watch's Settings app, then select Siri. Then, hit Siri Responses. Scroll down to the bottom of the page.

Quickly Pause Time By Typing To Siri

If you're having trouble speaking, you may either write a request to Siri or ask her to wait until you finish speaking.

1. Go to your Apple Watch's Settings.
2. To enable Type to Siri, go to Accessibility > Siri.
3. Tap Longer or Longest under Siri Pause Time to have Siri wait longer for you to complete speaking.

Eliminate All Siri Data

Apple servers save your requests for six months when you use Siri or dictation so they may enhance Siri's replies to you. Instead of linking your Apple ID or email address with your requests, a random identifier is used. These exchanges are permanently removed from the server.

1. Go to your Apple Watch's Settings.

2. To delete your Siri history, open Siri, then hit Siri History.

HOW TO USE YOUR APPLE WATCH AND WIRELESS HEADPHONES LIKE AIRPODS OR BEATS TO LISTEN TO AND REPLY TO ALERTS.

With compatible AirPods and Beats headphones, Siri can read aloud incoming alerts from a variety of applications without requiring you to unlock your iPhone. Siri listens after reading alerts and refrains from interrupting you, allowing you to react without even saying "Hey Siri."

Enable The Notification System

1. Depending on the kind of headphones you own, insert or place the linked headphones on your ears.
2. Connect them to the Apple Watch.
3. Go to your Apple Watch's Settings.
4. To enable Announce Notifications, go to Siri > Settings > Notifications.

Another option is to activate Announce Notifications in your iPhone's Settings app. Just go to Notifications > Announce Notifications.

Hint: Siri may read your unread alerts from the Notification Centre over the speaker on your Apple Watch or Bluetooth headphones. Simply choose "Read my notifications."

Make A Notification App Selection

You have the option to choose which applications may make announcements.

1. Depending on the kind of headphones you own, insert or place the linked headphones on your ears.
2. Go to your Apple Watch's Settings.
3. Scroll down under Siri > Announce Notifications and touch the applications you want to get audio alerts from.

Temporarily Turn Off Announce Notifications

1. The Control Centre may be accessed by pressing the side button.
2. Press the Notifications button for Announcements.
   You may activate it by tapping the Announce Notifications button once again.

Note: Removing AirPods disables the Announce Notifications button.

Get Back To Someone

"Reply, that's fantastic news," you could say.

After you say anything to Siri, she will repeat it and then ask for your confirmation before responding. (To disable the need to confirm before sending a reply, open your Apple Watch's Settings app, go to Siri > Announce Notifications, scroll down to the bottom, and enable Reply without Confirmation.)

Put An End To Siri Reading Notifications.

Here are some options for you:

- Use the words "stop" or "cancel" to communicate.
- Use the digital crown on your AirPods Max.

  Attention: To adjust the loudness of a notification, just spin the Digital Crown.

- For the AirPods Pro or AirPods 3rd generation, press the Force Sensor.
- For the second-generation AirPods, double-tap on any one of them.
- Take out one of your AirPods—the Pro, the 2nd or 3rd generation, or any of the other models.

You may enable Announce Notifications on your Apple Watch by opening the Settings app, navigating to Siri > Announce Notifications, and then turning them on if you forgot to do so during AirPods setup.

HOW TO USE APPLE WATCH'S SIRI TO ANNOUNCE INCOMING CALLS

Messages and other app alerts may be announced by Siri on headphones that are compatible with her. Announce Calls is compatible with third-party applications that are supported as well.

1. Go to your Apple Watch's Settings.
2. To enable Announce Calls, tap Siri.
3. You are prompted to answer incoming calls when the caller ID is shown. Put your hand up if you're available or down if you're not.

EXPLORE THE FACE GALLERY ON APPLE WATCH

The most convenient method to see all of the available watch faces is via the Face Gallery in the Apple Watch app. From the gallery, you may choose an intriguing face, personalize it, set the level of complexity, and then add it to your collection.

Bring Up The Face Gallery.

On an iPhone, launch the Apple Watch app and locate the Face Gallery option towards the bottom of the screen.

Pick Out Facial Characteristics

Select a face from the Face Gallery and then choose a property, such as color or style, by tapping on it.

To help you find the perfect design, the top face changes as you experiment with various alternatives.

Crank Up The Difficulty In The Face Gallery.

1. Select a face from the Face Gallery and then press the position of the complications (e.g., Top Left, Top Right, or Bottom).
2. To see the various complications for that position, swipe left or right. Tap on the one you choose.
3. Just go to the very top of the list and choose Off if you're not interested in that position's complications.

Add A Face

1. Simply touch on a face in the Face Gallery and customize it with the features and difficulties that suit your needs.
2. Press the Add button.

   Your Apple Watch will now have this face as part of your collection.

HOW TO CHANGE THE WATCH FACE ON YOUR APPLE WATCH

Customize the appearance and functionality of your Apple Watch face to suit your needs. Before adding a design to your collection, you may customize it by choosing colors and adding features. To see the correct timekeeping tools or to change things up, you may switch faces at any time.

The Apple Watch app's Face Gallery is the simplest method to peruse all of the face options, personalize one, and add it to your collection. If you don't have access to your iPhone, don't worry—you can change the face directly on your watch.

Pick Up A New Face For Your Watch

To change the watch face, press and hold the screen, then swipe to the desired face.

Hint: you can also swipe between different watch faces. Launch the Apple Watch's Settings app, go to Clock, and finally, enable Swipe to Switch Watch Face.

Swipe left or right to see other watch faces.

Simple

Edit

Add features to your watch face.

Make The Watch Face More Intricate.

To quickly access information from other applications you've installed, check the weather, see stock prices, or add extra features, called complexities, to select watch faces.

1. When the watch face is shown, press and hold the screen to bring up the Edit menu.
2. Complete the gesture by swiping left.

The last screen displays any issues that a face may provide.

3. To switch complications, tap on one to choose it, and then use the Digital Crown to select another, such as Activity or Heart Rate.
4. To save your modifications, hit the Digital Crown. Then, to switch to it, tap the face.

Complicating matters further are some of the applications available in the App Store.

Apple Watch's Complication Possibilities

Pressing a watch face complication will launch the majority of applications. Some intricacies display data from a single app, allowing you to quickly get the information you need. Problems with air quality, conditions, temperature, and other factors are all part of weather.

Several intricacies are shown by the following applications.

App	Available complications
Activity	Rings
	Timeline
Astronomy	Earth
	Moon
	Solar
	Solar System
Calendar	Today's Date
	Your Schedule
Compass	Compass
	Elevation
	Level
Compass Waypoints	Last Viewed Waypoint
	Saved Waypoints
	Parked Car Waypoint
Home	Home
	Grid Forecast
Maps	Maps
	Get Directions
Mindfulness	Mindfulness
	State of Mind

Reminders	Due Today	
	Reminders	
Sleep	Data	
	Data and Schedule	
	Sleep	
Stocks	Added Stocks	
	Last Viewed Stocks	
Time	Analog Seconds	
	Analog Time	
	Digital Seconds	
	Digital Time	
Timer	Added Timers	
	Timer	
Weather	Air Quality	
	Conditions	
	Humidity	
	Rain	
	Temperature	
	UV Index	
	Wind	
World Clock	Sunrise/Sunset	
	Added Locations	

HOW TO ENHANCE YOUR COLLECTION WITH A NEW WATCH FACE

Make your own set of unique faces, including variants on the same design.

1. Press and hold the screen while the present watch face is shown.
2. To add a new one, swipe left until you reach the end, and then press the plus sign.
3. Select a watch face by rotating the Digital Crown, and then press the Add button.

   Hint: Tap on a collection, such as New Watch Faces or Artists, to peruse watch faces in a particular genre.

The watch face may be customized after adding it.

Tap new, scroll to browse watch faces, then tap a face to add it.

Peruse Your Assortment

A quick look will reveal all of your watch faces.

1. Launch the Apple Watch on your iOS device.
2. To access your collection, press My Watch and then swipe down from My Faces.

You may change the sequence of your collection by going to My Faces, tapping Edit, and then dragging the Reorder icon next to a watch face.

Your collection may be rearranged in whatever order you choose on Apple Watch. To move the currently displayed watch face to the left or right, tap and hold the screen twice.

How To Delete A Face From Your Collection

1. Press and hold the screen while the present watch face is shown.
2. Locate the unwanted face by swiping up on it, and then press Remove.

Alternately, launch the Apple Watch app on your iPhone, go to the My Watch section, and then press Edit. Select all of the watch faces you want to remove, then hit the Delete button.

You have the option to re-add the watch face at a later time.

Swipe up to delete a watch face, then tap Remove.

Prioritize The Time Piece

1. Go to your Apple Watch's Settings.
2. Pull down the clock.
3. Press the +0 minute button and then use the Digital Crown to advance the watch by up to 59 minutes.

No other times (like World Clock) or alarms or alerts will be affected by this option; it just modifies the time that appears on the watch face.

HOW TO SHARE A WATCH FACE WITH YOUR COLLECTION

Collaborate with pals by sharing watch faces. Complications made by third parties or integrated into watchOS may also be considered shared faces.

Note: Someone else's Apple Watch running watchOS 7 or later is also required to get the watch face.

Share A Watch Face

1. Display the watch face you want to share on your Apple Watch.
2. Press and hold the screen to bring up the Share menu.
3. For any complexities you would want to keep private, press "Don't include" after tapping the name of the watch face.

4. Choose a receiver or go to Messages/Mail.

Just touch on Messages or Mail, then enter the recipient's name, the topic (Mail), and the message.

5. Select Send.

Additionally, you may go to the Apple Watch app, choose a watch face from your library or the Face Gallery, and then hit the Share icon. From there, you can select a sharing option.

Get A Face For Your Watch

Messages, Mail, or a web link may all be used to send you shared watch faces.

1. Get the shared watch face by opening an email, text, or link.
2. To add a shared watch face, touch on it.

If a third-party software offers a complicated watch face, you may download it from the software Store by tapping the price or Get. To get the watch face without the third-party complexity, you may alternatively choose to continue without this app.

CHAPTER NINE

HOW TO GET STARTED WITH APPLE FITNESS+

Health, interval training, yoga, core, cycling, strength, and a whole lot more are all part of the Apple Fitness+ library. If you're looking to enhance your general feeling of well-being, you may also try participating in guided meditations. These can be 5-, 10-, or 20-minute sessions.

Put on your Apple Watch as you work out, and it will sync with your daily activity data afterward and communicate metrics like calories burnt and heart rate with your iOS device while you exercise.

Note: Not all countries or areas offer Apple Fitness+.

Subscribe To Apple Fitness+ App

Apple Fitness+ requires a membership to exercise. Launch the Fitness app on your iOS device. Next,

choose Fitness+ from the menu on your iPhone. Click the "Free Trial" option and then follow the on-screen prompts.

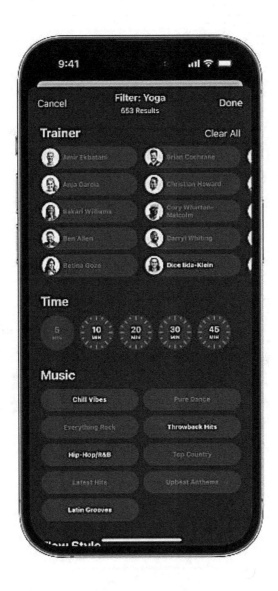

Pick A Routine And A Personal Trainer

When you're ready to go to the gym, open the Fitness app and pick a session or trainer. To assist you in making a selection, you may get a sample of each exercise along with facts like as the music type and playlist, whether or not the activity includes closed captions, and any necessary equipment.

During workouts with Apple Fitness+, each trainer brings their distinct personality, musical preferences, and training technique. Each trainer's bio and exercise routines are available for your perusal.

Examine Your Data

Make note of how far you've come on each of your rings while you work out. You can also see your heart rate and the number of calories you've burnt when exercising with your Apple Watch.

Each exercise has its own set of on-screen statistics, and you can see how you stack up against other users' measurements in the Burn Bar that appears for certain exercises. While you're working out, you may modify the displayed stats by tapping the screen.

Create A Custom Plan

Make a personalized exercise regimen that works with your busy schedule and keeps you motivated to reach your fitness objectives. press Fitness+, then press Build Your Plan. From there, you can choose the days you want to exercise, the duration of each session, and the sorts of exercises you wish to do (such as high-intensity interval training, yoga, strength training, meditation, and more).

HOW TO SUBSCRIBE TO APPLE FITNESS+

Apple Fitness+ may be subscribed to using the Fitness app on any Apple device, including the iPhone, iPad, and Apple TV. Apple Fitness+ is available as part of Apple One Premier, which allows you to combine your Apple services at a discounted rate. Refer to the Apple Support page on how to combine Apple subscriptions with Apple One.

Note: Not all countries or areas provide Apple Fitness+ and Apple One Premier.

What You Need To Use Apple Fitness+

Apple Watch Series 3 or later running watchOS 7.2 or later, in conjunction with an iPhone 6s or later running iOS 14.3 or later, is required to do an Apple Fitness+ exercise on an Apple Watch.

An iPhone 8 or later running iOS 16.1 or later is required to participate in an Apple Fitness+ exercise without an Apple Watch.

Important: If you don't have an Apple Watch, your workouts won't show you your heart rate or the number of calories you've burned.

If you own an Apple Watch or iPhone that is compatible with Apple Fitness+, you may utilize it throughout your exercises on:

- Apple device running iOS 14.3 or later
- Any Apple TV 4K or HD running tvOS 14.3 or later

Use an Apple Watch Series 4 or later running watchOS 10, an iPhone X or later running iOS 17, an iPad running iPadOS 17, and an Apple TV 4K or Apple TV HD running tvOS 17 to access the most recent Apple Fitness+ features.

Obtain The Exercise App.

Apple Fitness+ requires the Fitness app, which is available for iOS devices and Apple TV. The Fitness app is available for download on the App Store in case you don't already have it.

Apple Fitness+ Subscription

1. Boot up your iOS device and launch the Fitness app. After that, hit Fitness+ on your iPhone.
2. Select the "Free Trial" option, then enter your Apple ID and confirm your membership by following the on-screen prompts.

Cancel Your Apple Fitness+

1. Boot up your iOS device and launch the Fitness app. After that, press Summary on an iPhone. To access Apple Fitness+, press your profile image, then hit [account name].
2. To modify or terminate your membership, just follow the on-screen prompts.

Use Apple Family Sharing To Share Your Apple Fitness+ Membership.

You may utilize Family Sharing to let up to five additional family members use your Apple Fitness+ or Apple One Premier membership. If your family members have an Apple Watch Series 4 or later, they will automatically have access to Apple Fitness+ the first time they open the Fitness app once their membership starts. No action is required on their part. Apple Fitness+ is compatible with Apple TV and iPads, so even if a family member doesn't have an iPhone—maybe because someone else in the family set up an Apple Watch—they may still use it.

Note: If you do not want your Apple Fitness+ membership to be shared with a family group, you may remove them from the group.

DISCOVER THE BEST MEDITATIONS AND EXERCISES ON APPLE FITNESS+.

Discover your perfect exercise, meditation, or program with the aid of Apple Fitness+. You have the option to search for particular exercises or meditations, begin a program consisting of numerous episodes, organize and filter exercises by type, stack your preferred activities, get trainer advice, or choose a workout that is tailored to your activity level. Except for the 5-minute Mindful Cooldown and Core routines, all other exercise types may last anywhere from 15 to 45 minutes, and new routines are introduced weekly. Choose from five, ten, or twenty-minute meditations.

Peruse Exercises And Mindfulness Techniques

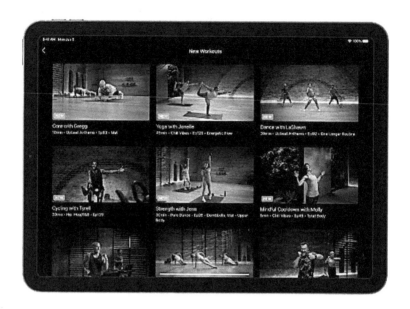

Based on your usual activities in the Apple Watch's Workout app and the applications you use most with the Health app, Apple Fitness+ will suggest exercises for you to complete. If you want to spice up your training regimen, Apple Fitness+ can even recommend new trainers and exercises.

1. Boot up your iOS device and launch the Fitness app. After that, hit Fitness+ on your iPhone.

2. Perform one of these tasks:
    - **Sort By Kind Of Activity:** Select an activity type from the list at the top of the screen by swiping left or right.

- **Listen To Exercise Programmes (iPhone Only):** If you own an Apple Watch, you can use it to play exercises designed for walking or running.

  After selecting Time to Walk or Time to Run, tap the Add button to add the episode to your Apple Watch. To access your additional episodes, launch the exercise app on your Apple Watch, go to Audio Workouts, scroll down to Library, and finally, hit the exercise. To access previous episodes, just scroll down, touch Time to Walk or Time to Run, and then use the Digital Crown to navigate.

- Discover highlighted activities by browsing the site's many categories, such as New Workouts, New Meditations, Beginners' Workouts, Popular, or Simple and Quick.

- You may browse exercises by trainer by scrolling down to Fitness+ Trainers, swiping left or right, and tapping on a trainer. You can then filter workouts by kind, duration, and music genre, as well as by trainer.

If you want to see all of the trainers, tap Show All.

- The more you use the Health app, the more you may peruse routines with your usual trainers and the sorts of workouts you often undertake on your Apple Watch or with other fitness applications that are compatible with it.
- Give it a go: To keep things interesting, try out workouts that are comparable to your current regimen but with various trainers and recommended sorts of exercises.
- Peruse My Collection: From either the exercise detail or workout summary page, you may access your stored workouts, meditations, stacks, and Custom Plans by scrolling down to My Library. Create a fitness program, store workouts for offline playback, or just keep track of your favorite exercises in My Library.

The checkmark symbol appears on the thumbnail of previously completed activities as you browse.

Tip: Using the Mindfulness app on your Apple Watch, you can listen to guided meditations if you have an Apple Fitness+ subscription.

Make Use Of Stacks To Merge Tasks

Stacks are a way to organize your exercises or meditations in Apple Fitness+ so you may do them in succession. You may blend your favorite hobbies into personalized lengthy workouts using stacks. An example of a stack might be a series of intensive exercises followed by a meditation to calm down.

Stack ...

Yoga with Jonelle
45min · Chill Vibes · Ep120

HIIT with Bakari
20min · Throwback Hits · Ep109

Meditation with Christian
5min · Resilience · Ep165

Let's Go

2 Workouts, 1 Meditation
Total: 70min

1. Boot up your iOS device and launch the Fitness app. After that, hit Fitness+ on your iPhone.
2. Select an action by tapping on it, and then hit the plus sign in the upper right.
3. Press the "Add to Stack" button.

   Hint: Another option is to touch and hold an activity before tapping the Add to Stack button.

4. After you've done adding exercises to your stack, you may perform one of the following by tapping the Stack button in the upper right corner:
   - Tap Let's Go to begin building your stack.
   - Stack your books in My Library: To add a stack to your library, first use the More Options option.
   - After naming the stack, hit the Save button.
   - Remove a task from your queue: Pick the action by swiping left, and then press Delete.
   - Rearrange the tasks on your to-do list: Activities may be rearranged by dragging the corresponding Reorder button.

- Get rid of your pile: Press the Clear Stack button after tapping the More Options icon.
- Hit Let's Go to begin the next action in your stack, or hit Done to go back to Apple Fitness+, once you finish an activity in your stack.

Receive Advice From A Trainer

When you sign up for Apple Fitness+, you'll get access to quick films with tips for being active and mindful, demonstrations of how to improve your technique, and guidance from experts to help you reach your objectives.

Note: Trainer Tips are currently unavailable in certain areas or countries.

1. Boot up your iOS device and launch the Fitness app. After that, hit Fitness+ on your iPhone.
2. To see the trainer tip, scroll down to the section and touch on the tip.

   Or, to see all of the trainer recommendations at once, just touch Show All.

Note: Each week brings a fresh tip.

Workouts And Meditations May Be Sorted And Filtered.

Sorting and filtering activities by trainer, duration, music genre, and more makes it easy to locate what you're searching for, whether it's a rowing session or a meditation session.

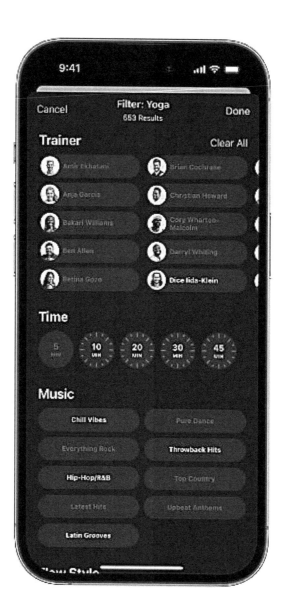

204

1. Boot up your iOS device and launch the Fitness app. After that, hit Fitness+ on your iPhone.
2. Choose an activity category, and then proceed with one of these options:
   - **Sorting Tasks:** Choose an option, such as Trainer or Time, by tapping Sort.
   - **Purification Processes:** After that, choose the filter(s) you want to use by tapping the Filter button.

   There are no applicable activities for a given filter if it is not selectable.

Try A Multi-Episode Programme For Meditation Or Exercise.

1. Boot up your iOS device and launch the Fitness app. After that, hit Fitness+ on your iPhone.
2. Choose an option from these:
   - **Fitness Regimens:** Tap Show All after scrolling to Workout Programmes.
   - **Programs For Meditation:** Find Meditation Programmes and press the Show All button.
3. Press on a show.

The program's training kinds and episode count are shown on each tile.

4. Perform one of these tasks:
   - **See The Show In Action:** Tap Take a look at the film to get a feel for the program's aims and the exercises you may expect to complete. For additional information, you can also read up on the program.
   - **Add An Episode To Your My Library:** You can do that by tapping the Add button next to it or by tapping the Add All button at the bottom of the screen.
   - **Launch The Show's Latest Episode:** After finding an episode you want to work out to, touch the button to start.

After finishing an episode, the next one will appear automatically under Next Workout to help you stay on track, but you are free to choose any episode whenever you want.

HOW TO START AN APPLE FITNESS+ WORKOUT OR MEDITATION

With Apple Fitness+, you can begin a meditation or exercise session right from your iOS device. You may push yourself to new limits with Apple Fitness+

routines, whether you're a beginner or simply want to do the same old thing over and over again. You have the freedom to start an exercise, stop it whenever you want, and then evaluate it after it's over.

Take Up Some Exercise Or Meditation

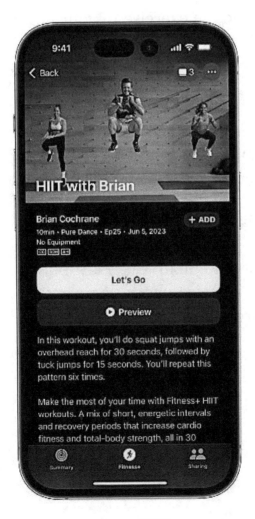

1. Launch the app for fitness. After that, hit Fitness+ on your iPhone.
2. Choose a meditation or exercise from the meditation or exercise categories (such as Popular or Guest Trainer Series) or tap on an activity type at the top of the screen.
3. Perform one of these tasks:
   - To save the exercise to your library, just hit the "Add Workout" button.
   - Tap Preview to see the activity in action.

     The activity's playlist is also shown. To access the playlist on Apple Music, tap Listen in Music if you have an Apple Music subscription.

   - To begin an activity, press the button that says "Start Activity" or, for iOS devices, press and hold the Play button. For the most precise data, choose Run or Walk before beginning a treadmill exercise.

     You may begin the activity even if you don't have your Apple Watch on, but it won't track your stats (like calories burnt). To begin the exercise, touch the "Work Out Without Watch" button.

To transmit your exercise to a TV HomePod or any other device that supports AirPlay 2.0, all you have to do is touch the screen while you're exercising and then push the AirPlay button.

Starting a meditation or exercise routine is also possible on Apple TV.

Additional trainers show you how to make each activity simpler or more difficult in every program. Alternately, trainers may suggest ways to adapt exercises, such as doing the motion using just your body weight rather than dumbbells.

Break And Go Back To Exercising Or Meditating

Whether it's the device playing the exercise or your Apple Watch, you can halt it whenever you want.

- Perform one of these actions on your Apple Watch:
  - Stop what you're doing by simultaneously pressing the side button and the Digital Crown. Pressing the Pause button follows a left or right swipe.

- Pressing the side button and the Digital Crown simultaneously, swiping right and tapping Resume, or swiping left and tapping the Play button are all ways to resume activity.
- Follow these steps on your iOS device:
  - Stop what you're doing: Press and hold the screen until you see the Pause button.
  - Return to a previous task: Press the Play button.

Wrap Up A Meditation Or Exercise Session And Reflect On It.

Either the device currently playing the exercise or your Apple Watch may be used to terminate a meditation or workout.

- Select End, then press End Workout, on the Apple Watch.

  The results of your exercise are shown below. Press the Done button to get back to the Workout app.

- If you're using an iOS device, you may end your workout by tapping the End button.

The results of your exercise are shown below. To save the activity to your library, touch the Add button. To share the activity, hit the Share button. To choose a cooldown exercise, tap Mindful Cooldown. To get back to Apple Fitness+, tap Done.

Afterward, you may get your exercise report inside the iPhone Fitness app.

The checkmark indicator on the thumbnail of a class will show in the list of workouts after you've completed it.

HOW TO CREATE A CUSTOM PLAN IN APPLE FITNESS+

To ensure that you achieve your fitness objectives, you have the option to design a personalized plan that works around your schedule. Incorporate high-intensity interval training (HIIT), yoga, weight training, meditation, and many more into your personalized training program.

Create Your Plans

1. Boot up your iOS device and launch the Fitness app. After that, hit Fitness+ on your iPhone.

2. After that, tap on "Build Your Plan," and then:
   - Choose your timetable for the week: Mark the days when you would want to exercise.
   - Choose the entire time you spend exercising: Under Total Time Per Day, touch a time interval.
   - Choose the duration of your plan: Press a time next to Plan Length.
   - Just choose the things you're interested in doing: Select up to five tasks.

To include additional exercises in your Custom Plan, you may have to extend the overall time spent exercising and add more training days to your weekly schedule.

3. After tapping Review Plan, you may perform one of these things:
   - Deciding when to begin the plan is: Tap on a beginning date that appears under the Review Plan.
   - Revise the steps outlined in your strategy: To see what kinds of things are on your agenda for the week, swipe left on your calendar.

     To modify the kind and parameters of an activity, touch on it and then hit Update.

   - If you'd like to add an activity to one of the days in your schedule, you may do so by swiping left on that day and then tapping Add. To edit the activity's parameters and type, touch on it, and then hit the Add button.
   - Personalize your workouts and playlists: Choose the trainers and music genres you'd want to hear in your plan by tapping on the corresponding buttons.

4. Finally, hit the Create Plan button.

Modify Your Custom Plan

Depending on your tastes, you may modify the pre-selected activities once you've made your Custom Plan.

1. Boot up your iOS device and launch the Fitness app. After that, hit Fitness+ on your iPhone.
2. Press the View Plan button, and then choose an option:
   - Your Custom Plan may be renamed: To rename the plan, use the More Options option.
   - Take a look at your Custom Plan's exercises: You can see every single thing you have planned for each week by swiping left.
   - Simply choose an activity, hit the Swap option that appears next to it, and then select a different routine to swap it out for.

      Note: Exercise swaps are only available on the days when you have planned activities.

Embark On A Personal Plan

1. Boot up your iOS device and launch the Fitness app. After that, hit Fitness+ on your iPhone.
2. To begin, choose Your Plan from the menu, then hit the Let's Go button.

Note: You will get push notifications on your iPhone to initiate your Custom Plan.

Delete Your Custom Plan

1. Boot up your iOS device and launch the Fitness app. After that, hit Fitness+ on your iPhone.
2. After selecting View Plan, go to the More Options menu, and finally, choose End Plan.

You have unlimited opportunities to restore a deleted Custom Plan. Go to My Library, then choose Custom Plans. Then, choose the plan that appears underneath Previous Custom Plans and tap on it. Finally, press on Repeat Plan.

HOW TO WORK OUT TOGETHER USING SHAREPLAY

You and up to thirty-two of your closest friends may get a workout in together with SharePlay Group Workouts. Initiate a Group Workout in the Fitness app while simultaneously starting a FaceTime chat on your iOS device.

While doing high-intensity interval training (HIIT), treadmill running, cycling, or rowing, you and your friends can control the music and cheer each other on. You can also see when someone closes an activity ring and receive alerts when someone goes ahead of the group on the Burn Bar.

To participate in Apple Fitness+ group workouts, you'll need one of the following iOS devices: Any device running iOS 15.1 or later, including iPhones, iPads, and iPod touches. Requires macOS 12.1 or later for playback on Mac. There may be regional or national restrictions on the availability of FaceTime or its capabilities, as well as other Apple services. To use an Apple Watch while exercising, you need a Series 4 or later model running watchOS 8.1 or later.

Launch A Group Workout On Your Ios Device With Facetime

1. Launch a FaceTime meeting.
2. Boot up your iOS device and launch the Fitness app. Next, choose Fitness+ on your iPhone.

If the Fitness app isn't already installed on your smartphone, you may get it from the App Store.

3. After you've chosen a workout and started it, you may start it with all the others on the call by tapping the SharePlay button. (When asked to utilize SharePlay, additional callers may need to press Open before they can join the Group Workout.)

All participants on the call with access will hear the exercise music begin playing simultaneously. Anyone without access is requested to get it (either by subscribing or, if offered, by trying it out for free).

The exercise may be played or paused by anybody using the playback controls on their device, including the Apple Watch.

On iOS devices, you may stop an exercise before it finishes by tapping the X in the upper left corner. Press End after swiping right on the Apple Watch.

Launch A Group Workout From Your iOS Device's Fitness App.

1. Boot up your iOS device and launch the Fitness app. Next, choose Fitness+ on your iPhone.

   If the Fitness app isn't already installed on your smartphone, you may get it from the App Store.

2. After choosing a workout, go to the More Options menu and hit the SharePlay option.

3. After adding your desired workout partners to the "To" section, just hit the "FaceTime" button.

4. Press the "Let's Begin" button after the FaceTime connection has connected.

   To join in on the exercise, the receiver has to touch the workout's title on the top of the FaceTime interface and then hit Open. All participants on the call with access will hear the exercise music begin playing simultaneously. Anyone without access is requested to get it (either by subscribing or, if offered, by trying it out for free).

   The exercise may be played or paused by anybody using the playback controls on their device, including the Apple Watch.

On iOS devices, you may stop an exercise before it finishes by tapping the X in the upper left corner. Press End after swiping right on the Apple Watch.

HOW TO MODIFY THE DISPLAY SETTINGS FOR YOUR APPLE FITNESS+ MEDITATION OR EXERCISE SESSION.

Modify Onscreen Metrics

Your smartphone will display your progress for each of your rings in real-time while you exercise. Wearing an Apple Watch while exercising allows you to monitor not just your heart rate but also the number of calories you burn.

You may see how your stats compare to other users who have completed the program before you on some routines that use the Burn Bar. A higher position on the Burn Bar indicates a greater caloric expenditure. In addition to other stats, your exercise report now includes your position on the Burn Bar.

While exercising, you may customize the metrics shown on the screen by using Apple Watch. When you login in with your Apple ID on any of your Apple devices, the settings for your metrics will sync inside the Fitness app.

Notably, Fitness+ members may now get real-time personal stats from their Apple Watch on compatible monitors when using AirPlay to view their exercises.

1. Press the Metrics button while you're exercising.
2. Choose an option from these:
   - Click the "Show Metrics" button to disable all metrics.

     While your measurements are still being gathered, they will not be shown on the screen.

   - Choose from three different ways to see the time: off, shown as elapsed time, and shown as remaining time.

     Turning off Your workout's interval timer is still visible.

- Exit the Burn Bar: Exit the Burn Bar.

  You won't be able to view your position after your exercise is over or add your workout to the community burn bar if you disable the Burn Bar.

Disable Auto Focus

Apple Fitness+ gives you the option to listen to music or the trainer's voice as you work out.

Note: You'll need iOS 17.2 or later to access Audio Focus. It won't function with the Time to Walk or Time to Run exercises, nor with audio or video meditations.

Select Trainer or Music from the list that appears when you hit the More Options button while exercising.

Turn On Audio Hints

During your exercise, you have the option to activate audio suggestions, which provide extra spoken signals to explain the trainer's movements.

1. Click the "More Options" button while you're exercising.
2. Pick Audio Hints and then turn them on.

You may change the pace by tapping Audio Hints again and then selecting the speed you want.

Enable Closed Captioning And Subtitles.

Regular captions and SDH subtitles are available for all Apple Fitness+ exercises and meditations. Just underneath the workout's duration, genre, and date uploaded, you'll notice whether it has closed captioning or SDH.

Select a language by tapping the Subtitles button while exercising.

CHAPTER TEN

HOW TO USE ASSITIVETOUCH ON APPLE WATCH

If you have trouble touching the screen or tapping the buttons on your Apple Watch, AssistiveTouch may assist. Thanks to its integrated sensors, the Apple Watch can respond to calls, move an on-screen pointer, and open a menu with only the wave of a wrist.

Among other things, you may use AssistiveTouch gestures to do the following:

- Press the screen
- Use the on-screen controls and digital crown
- Switch between displays with a swipe.
- Depress the button on the side
- Use the App Switcher, Control Centre, and Notification Centre
- Feature applications
- Make payment with Apple Pay
- Verify the action of pressing the side button twice
- Bring up Siri
- Take advantage of an expedited Siri process

Note: Before you activate AssistiveTouch, you should know that the Apple Watch Series 9 does not support the universal double tap gesture.

Set Up AssistiveTouch

1. Go to your Apple Watch's Settings.
2. Accessibility > AssistiveTouch is where you'll find the toggle to activate the feature.
3. To activate Hand Gestures, tap on that feature.

   Tip: Use the "Learn more" button under the "Hand Gestures" toggle to see a list of gestures and their respective explanations. You may learn and master any motion by tapping on it, and an interactive animation will teach you the steps.

Alternatively, you may activate AssistiveTouch by opening the Apple Watch app on your iPhone, tapping My Watch, and then navigating to Accessibility > AssistiveTouch.

Use AssistiveTouch With Apple Watch

Here are the default motions for navigating your Apple Watch with AssistiveTouch and Hand motions enabled:

- Press: Continue
- Press and hold: Return
- Knock: Press
- Pull up the menu of options with a double-clench

To demonstrate how to utilize AssistiveTouch with the Activity app, these are the steps to take while the Meridian watch face is displayed:

1. To activate AssistiveTouch, double-press. Around the Music's complexity, a spotlight emerges.
2. To access the Activity complication, press three times. Then, squeeze to tap it.
3. You may access the Action Menu by double-pressing the screen when the Activity app launches.
4. Select the System action with a single press, the Scroll Up action with a second tap, and finally, click to pick it.
5. Press the space bar to go to the next screen. The Action Menu will appear when you double-tap.
6. To get to the next step, tap; to return to the previous one, double tap.
7. To get back to the watch face, press and hold the crown once.

Use The Motion Pointer

Using the Motion Pointer, you may tilt your Apple Watch up and down and side to side to operate it, in addition to tapping and gripping. For instance, here's how to utilize the Motion Pointer in the Stopwatch app:

1. To enable AssistiveTouch, double-press when the watch face is visible.
2. To reveal the Action Menu, double-click once more.
   An action called Press Crown will be chosen.
3. To access the Home screen, press and hold the Crown icon.
4. If you want to access the Action Menu, double-press the screen twice. Then, to access the Interaction action, tap and hold.
   Choose the Motion Pointer option.
5. Press the button to activate the motion pointer.
   On the screen, a pointer shows up.
6. Drag the pointer down to the screen's edge by tilting the watch.
7. To launch the Stopwatch app, briefly hover your mouse over its icon.
8. To press the start button, keep your pointer over it.

9. Press the crown to return to the watch face; to access the Action Menu, double-press and then clench.

Use Quick Actions

When you see an alert on your Apple Watch, you can reply quickly. For instance, a notification informs you that you may answer a call with a double-tap when one is arriving. In addition, when your Apple Watch senses motion that is similar to a workout, you may start a workout with the press of a button, and while the viewfinder and shutter button are visible in the Camera app, you can utilize fast actions to snooze or stop the timer. The following steps will enable or disable fast actions:

1. Go to your Apple Watch's Settings.
2. Select a setting under Accessibility > Quick Actions.

Quick actions may be made accessible always, just while AssistiveTouch is enabled, or disabled. There are two more options: Full appearance (which highlights the action button and displays a banner) and Minimal appearance (which highlights the action button without the banner).

Tip: By tapping "Try it out," you may practice the rapid actions gesture.

Customise AssistiveTouch To Your Liking

You can modify the sensitivity of the Motion Pointer, and alter the actions that are assigned to tapping, clenching, and the Movement Pointer motions.

To use the AssistiveTouch feature, open the Apple Watch's Settings app and go to Accessibility. After that, you may perform one of the following:

- Alter the motions to your liking by going to Hand motions, tapping a gesture, and then selecting an activity or a Siri shortcut.
- Select Motion Pointer from the menu, and then tweak the sensitivity, activation time, movement tolerance, and hot edges settings to your liking.
- Style of scanning: Pick between Automatic scanning, in which each action is highlighted automatically, or Manual scanning, in which you transition between them using gestures.
- To make the highlight bolder, go to the appearance menu and choose High Contrast. To change the color of the highlight, tap Colour.

- Personalize the menu by adding your preferred actions, resizing the Action Menu, and modifying the auto-scroll speed.
- To enable AssistiveTouch, toggle it on. This will allow you to confirm payments using the passcode or whenever you need to double-click the side button.

Other options include opening the Apple Watch app on an iPhone, tapping My Watch, and then navigating to Accessibility > AssistiveTouch.

HOW TO USE BLUETOOTH KEYBOARD WITH VOICEOVER ON APPLE WATCH

To manage VoiceOver output, you may link a Bluetooth keyboard. Press and hold the modifier keys on your keyboard while you text to use VoiceOver on your Apple Watch.

Pair A Wireless Keyboard

1. Go to your Apple Watch's Settings.
2. Accessibility > VoiceOver > Keyboards is the place to go.
3. Pair the keyboard by going to the settings menu, scrolling down to the bottom, and tapping on the keyboard under the Devices section.

Modify The Keypad Preferences

1. Go to your Apple Watch's Settings.
2. Accessibility > VoiceOver > Keyboards is the place to go.
3. Choose from the following options:

Setting	Description
Phonetic feedback	Choose to hear characters and phonetics or phonetics only.
Typing feedback	Choose to hear characters, words, or characters and words as you type on the Bluetooth keyboard.
Modifier keys	Choose the modifier keys that must be pressed on a hardware keyboard to activate VoiceOver key commands. Options are Control + Option and Caps Lock.
Keyboard interaction time	Set the amount of time to wait before VoiceOver can start Slide to Type or make use of alternative keys on the software keyboard. Use the plus and minus buttons to adjust interaction time from zero to four seconds.

Use The Keys To Navigate

When using a Bluetooth keyboard, press the corresponding keys to navigate.

Setting	Action
Right Arrow key	Move to next item.
Left Arrow key	Move to previous item.
Modifier key + Down Arrow key	Read out character or phonetics of selected item from left to right.
Modifier key + Up Arrow key	Read out character or phonetics of selected item from right to left.
Modifier key + Space bar	Tap selected item.

HOW TO MODIFY APPLE WATCH'S FONT, SIZE, AND OTHER AESTHETIC SETTINGS

To enhance your interaction with on-screen elements, you have the option to change the font size and other settings.

Resize The Font

1. The Control Centre may be accessed by pressing the side button.
2. Just spin the Digital Crown to get the right size by tapping the Adjust Text Size button.

Make A Selection About The Appearance Of Text And Other Resources.

To alter the visual presentation of elements on the screen, you can apply several styles, such as bold text, grayscale, and more. Go to your Apple Watch's Settings, then touch on Accessibility. From there, you may toggle the following features on and off:

- Labels: On or Off

  To see an extra position indication, enable button labels. When you enable labels, you will see a one (1) for activated choices and a zero (0) for deactivated ones.

- Reduce transparency

  Legibility is improved with certain backdrops when transparency is reduced.

- Sharpen the picture

  To make the app's foreground and background colors stand out more, toggle this on.

- A variety of color filters

  For those who have trouble seeing the text on their watch screen or who are colorblind, color filters may be a great aid.

- Size of the text

- Highlighted text

Alternatively, you may access this feature by opening the Apple Watch app on your iPhone, tapping My Watch, and then selecting Accessibility.

Note: For the bold and grayscale text modifications to take effect, restart your Apple Watch.

Minimal Animation

Reduce the amount of movement you see on the Home Screen and when applications launch and exit.

1. Go to your Apple Watch's Settings.
2. Press the "Reduce Motion" button in the Accessibility menu.

Alternatively, you may activate Reduce Motion by opening the Apple Watch app on your iPhone, tapping My Watch, and then navigating to Accessibility > Reduce Motion.

Tip: Use grid view on the Home Screen with Reduce Motion enabled, and you'll see that all of the app icons are uniform in size.

HOW TO SET UP AND USE RTT ON APPLE WATCH

A technique known as real-time text (RTT) allows you to send audio along with your text input. If you're having trouble hearing or speaking, but still want to stay connected even when you're not near your iPhone, the Apple Watch with cellular can communicate via RTT. No other devices are needed since the Apple Watch utilizes its built-in Software RTT, which can be configured in the Apple Watch app.

Note: Not all carriers or areas provide RTT support. In the event of an emergency, the Apple Watch may notify the operator by sending a series of specific characters or tones while in the US. Where you are may affect whether or not the operator can hear or react to these tones. It is not Apple's responsibility to ensure that the operator can receive or answer an RTT call.

Turn On RTT

1. Launch the Apple Watch on your iOS device.
2. Go to Accessibility > RTT on My Watch, then toggle RTT on.
3. To set up a relay call using RTT, tap Relay Number and provide the desired number.

4. Enable the Send option Send every character instantly as you write. To finish sending messages, turn off the option.

Place An RTT Call

1. Boot up your Apple Watch and launch the Phone app.
2. Select Contacts and navigate through them with the Digital Crown.
3. After selecting the desired contact, scroll down and press the RTT button.
4. Just scribble away, choose a response from the selection, or hit "emoji" to send.

   Note: Not all languages are supported by Scribble.

   Apple Watch displays text like a Messages chat.

   Important: If the other party on the call does not have RTT enabled, you will be alerted.

Take A Call From An RTT

1. You may view who's calling by raising your wrist when you hear or feel the call notice.
2. Press the RTT button after tapping the Answer button and scrolling down.

3. Just scribble away, choose a response from the selection, or hit "emoji" to send.

Note: Not all languages are supported by Scribble.

Change Pre-Defined Responses

You can respond to an RTT call on Apple Watch with a single touch, whether you're making or receiving the call. Here are the procedures you need to take to make your replies:

1. Launch the Apple Watch on your iOS device.
2. Press My Watch, then choose Accessibility > RTT. Finally, press Default Replies.
3. Select "Add reply," type in your response, and then select "Done."

   Hint: You may usually signal to the other person that you're prepared to receive their response by ending your reply with "GA" (go ahead).

On the Default Answers screen, press Edit to modify or remove previous answers or rearrange their order.

HOW TO USE ACCESSIBILITY FEATURES WITH SIRI ON APPLE WATCH

When first setting up your Apple Watch's accessibility capabilities, Siri is usually the best bet. Use Siri as your intelligent personal assistant, launch applications, and toggle a plethora of settings.

Siri: If you want to use VoiceOver, ask Siri to say "Turn on VoiceOver" or "Turn off VoiceOver."

When you use VoiceOver, Siri will read out more text than what you see on the screen. Alternatively, you may utilize VoiceOver to make Siri's on-screen content audible.

Determine The Time That Siri Waits For You To Complete Speaking.

1. Go to your Apple Watch's Settings.
2. To change the Siri Pause Time, choose Accessibility > Siri. Scroll down and select Default, Longer, or Longest.

Instead Of Talking To Siri, Just Type

With Siri, you don't even need to talk. To use Siri by typing instead of speaking, follow these instructions.

1. Go to your Apple Watch's Settings.

2. To enable Type to Siri, go to Accessibility > Siri.

HOW TO RESTART APPLE WATCH

Restarting your Apple Watch and the iPhone it is connected to may fix most issues.

Restart Your Apple Watch

The Apple Watch Must Be Turned Off: To bring up the sliders, press and hold the side button. Then, press the Power button. Finally, drag the Power Off slider to the right.

Turn On Your Apple Watch: Press and hold the side button on your Apple Watch until the Apple logo shows up. This will turn on your watch.

Digital Crown

Side button

Note: While your Apple Watch is charging, you are unable to restart it.

Restart The Paired iPhone

- **Turn Off Your iPhone:** If your iPhone has Face ID, you can power it off by holding down the side button and a volume button simultaneously and then dragging the slider to the right. If your model doesn't have Face ID, you can still access the slider by pressing and holding the top or side button until it displays. Then, just move it to the right. You may also get the Shut Down option in any model by going to Settings > General.

- **Turn On Your iPhone:** Press and hold the side or top button on your iPhone until you see the Apple logo. This will turn on your device.

Get The Apple Watch To Start Up Again

Forcing an Apple Watch restart may be necessary if you are unable to power down the device or if the issue persists. This should only be done if restarting your Apple Watch fails.

Pressing and holding the side button and the Digital Crown simultaneously for 10 seconds, or until you see the Apple logo, will forcibly restart the device.

IF YOU FORGET YOUR APPLE WATCH PASSCODE

You may reset your Apple Watch and set it up again from your iPhone or Apple Watch if it becomes deactivated due to forgetting or repeatedly entering the wrong passcode.

Note: Remember to enable Erase Data on your Apple Watch. After 10 unsuccessful tries at entering the password, all data on the watch will be destroyed.

Reset Your Apple Watch

1. Once your Apple Watch is connected to its charger, you may access the sliders by pressing and holding the side button.
2. The Erase all content and settings page will appear when you press and hold the Digital Crown.
3. To confirm, touch Reset again after tapping Reset.
4. Once the procedure is complete, you will need to reset your watch. Back up your data and restore it when prompted.

Reset Your Apple Watch By Connecting It To Your iPhone.

1. Locate My Watch in the Apple Watch app on your iPhone.
2. Press Reset after tapping General and swiping down.
3. To confirm, press Erase All Content and Settings after tapping Erase Apple Watch Content and Settings.
4. Your cellular plan is up for grabs if your Apple Watch has one.
   - If you would want to reconnect your Apple Watch and iPhone, be sure to retain your plan.

- To disconnect your Apple Watch from your cellular service or to connect it to another iPhone, just remove your plan. (Try contacting your service provider to terminate your membership.)

5. Once the procedure is complete, you will need to reset your watch. Back up your data and restore it when prompted.

This method of erasing the Apple Watch activates the Activation Lock. Protect your Apple ID and password against unauthorized access with Activation Lock.

- Take your Apple Watch off the iPhone's charging dock.
- Connect your Apple Watch to a brand-new iPhone and get to work.
- Locate Me cannot be enabled on this device.

HOW TO RECOVER APPLE WATCH

If you see an animation on your Apple Watch depicting the two devices being brought together, here's what you need to do:

1. Bring your Apple Watch close to your iPhone. For this to work, your iPhone must have the latest iOS version, be unlocked, and be connected to Wi-Fi with Bluetooth enabled.

2. Locate the charging port for your Apple Watch.

3. To pair your Apple Watch with an iPhone, just double-click the side button on your wristwatch and then follow the on-screen instructions.

HOW TO RESTORE APPLE WATCH FROM A BACKUP

You may restore your Apple Watch from a backup that is automatically saved to your associated iPhone. Backing up your iPhone to iCloud or a computer also backs up your Apple Watch. You won't be able to access the data in your iCloud backups.

Apple Watch Backup And Restoration

- Prepare a backup of your Apple Watch: When synced with an iPhone, all data stored on the Apple Watch is automatically backed up to the iPhone in real-time. A backup is performed before unpairing the devices.

- Pick "Restore from Backup" and then pick an iPhone backup to restore your Apple Watch from if you re-pair your watch with the same iPhone or buy a new Apple Watch.

When a family member's Apple Watch is plugged into power and a Wi-Fi network, it automatically backs up to the family member's iCloud account. Navigate to [account name] > iCloud > iCloud Backups in the Settings app on the managed Apple Watch. From there, deactivate iCloud Backups for that watch.

HOW TO UPDATE APPLE WATCH SOFTWARE

By using the Apple Watch app on your iPhone, you can easily check for software upgrades for your Apple Watch.

Locate And Apply Any Available Software Patches.

1. Launch the Apple Watch on your iOS device.
2. To check whether an update is available, press the Download and Install button after tapping My Watch. Then, click on General > Software Update.

For another option, you may access the Settings app on your Apple Watch. From there, go to General > Software Update.

CHAPTER ELEVEN

TIPS AND TRICKS

1. Return To The Clock

It doesn't need to display the time every time you raise your wrist if you have an app that you would like to show. You can change the on-screen app by going to Settings > General > Return to Clock, regardless of whether your screen is always on or not.

Find the part that says "On Screen Raise Show Last" and scroll down to it. You have the option to select Always, Within 1 Hour of Last Use, Within 2 Minutes of Last Use, or While in Sessions.

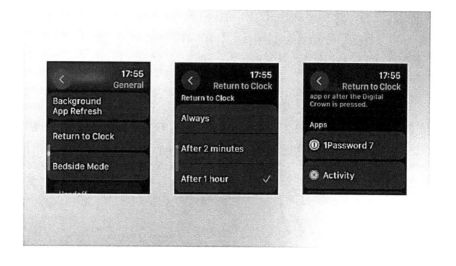

2. Size Up The Text That Appears On The Screen

Apple has made the accessibility setting available in case you want a larger font on your rather tiny gadget. To customize the brightness, go to Settings > Display & Brightness.

If you'd rather see the time displayed in big numbers, you have the option to select a specialized Big Text watch face.

3. Turn Off Notifications With Your Hand

Keep the Watch from waking up the neighbors with its blaring notifications by turning off the sound feature.

If it goes off in an unexpected spot, you can quickly silence it by covering the screen for three seconds or longer. Navigate to My Watch > Gestures > Cover to Mute in the Apple Watch app on your iPhone to enable the setting.

4. Secretly Remove Watch Applications

Go to the My Watch area of the Apple Watch app on your iPhone if you would like to hide all third-party apps from your Apple Watch. Find "Installed on Apple Watch" at the bottom of the page. Toggle the apps you wish to remove to the off position by tapping on them. Unless you also remove them from your iPhone, these apps will be loaded on your Watch even after you remove their interfaces.

5. Use Your Watch To Locate your iPhone

Is your iPhone missing? Lucky for you, the Apple Watch can direct you to its whereabouts. Press the side button on your Apple Watch. Here you may make it sound so you can find it easier by tapping the blue Ping button on the iPhone.

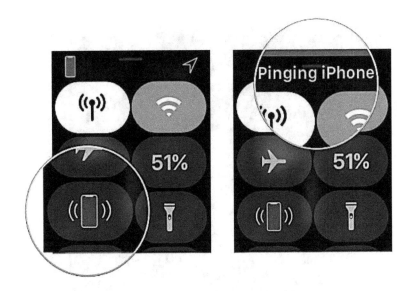

6. Zoom And Voiceover Are Easily Accessible.

Make sure your Apple Watch has all of your iPhone's critical features, like Zoom and VoiceOver, with ease. To make Zoom or VoiceOver launch automatically, enable the Accessibility shortcut (three clicks). Choose My Watch > Accessibility > Accessibility Shortcut from the Apple Watch app on your iPhone to accomplish this. This is where you may customize which ones will activate automatically when you triple-click.

You can also ask your Watch to activate or deactivate VoiceOver using Siri's voice commands.

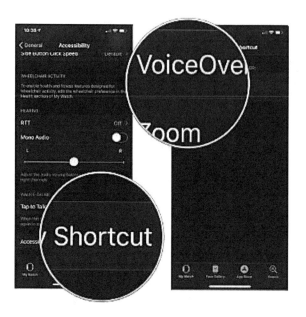

7. Take A Screenshot

You can capture screenshots of your Activity achievements or other creative creations you make on Digital Touch. Pressing the side button and the Digital Crown at the same time is all it takes to snap a screenshot.

8. Restart The Apple Watch By Force.

If your Watch starts acting up, you may disable it by tapping and holding the side button until you see the emergency instructions. To turn off the power, press and hold the power button located in the upper right corner. Holding the side button and

Digital Crown for 10 seconds or until you see the Apple logo can forcibly reset your Watch if it has completely frozen.

9. Save Your Watch Faces

With the use of Force Touch on the Watch screen, you may personalize the preset faces provided by Apple and even store your faces for later use. In that case, repeat the process of Force Touching the Watch screen, swiping left, and tapping the New button. Now that you've updated your watch face, you may personalize it to your liking.

Drag up to remove a personalized watch face.

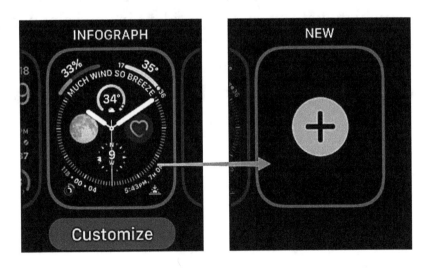

10. Make Your Watch Tick Faster By Five Minutes.

Your Apple Watch can help you remain punctual for all of your appointments and meetings if that's something you value. Are you someone who values punctuality? There will be no impact on your alarms, alerts, or time zones when you manually adjust the watch face to show five minutes faster (or more). It shows up on the face of your Watch. Simply go to the Settings menu, choose Clock, and then press +0 min. Then, use the digital crown to set the time forward by up to 59 minutes.

11. Disable The Snooze Feature On Your Alarms.

Turning off the snooze feature will wake you up immediately if you're not confident in your ability to get up at the appointed hour. To modify the alarm time, open the Alarm app on your smartphone. If you want to force yourself to get going, you may toggle the snooze option.

12. Prepare Replies For Personalized Messages In Advance

While most Apple Watches do not have a built-in keyboard, you can save some pre-written replies on your iPhone and then touch on them to send them automatically when you are in a discussion. Navigate to My Watch > Messages > Default Replies in the Apple Watch app to do this. Feel free to make changes to the list and include or exclude pre-written replies whenever you choose.

13. Use Force Touch In Messages To Share Your Location

Are you interested in sharing your precise whereabouts with a pal when you're out and about? Tap the App Store icon in your Messages discussion. Then, find the green disclose Location option. Either disclose your location or ask the other person to do the same.

14. Put A Call On Hold Until You Locate Your iPhone.

The Apple Watch may seem futuristic, but it's not always a practical means to make or receive calls. If you get a call on your Watch and want to answer it, but your phone isn't within easy reach, you may put the call on hold until you can locate your device by tapping Answer on your iPhone. The other party will experience a continuous tone till you reach your iPhone.

15.   Activate The Talkie-Toy

You can communicate with other Apple Watch users with the Walkie-Talkie function, but you have to enable it. On your Watch, open the Walkie-Talkie app and turn on the Available toggle. If you don't, the tool won't work for anybody trying to contact you.

www.ingramcontent.com/pod-product-compliance
Lightning Source LLC
LaVergne TN
LVHW051443050326
832903LV00030BD/3217